Praise for *The Impossible Mile*

"Johnny Agar is a true inspiration as a person and an athlete. Where most might see nothing but obstacles, he sees nothing but opportunities. Johnny's commitment to pursuing his dreams and sharing his journey along the way is a tremendous gift to us all."

—Michael Phelps, most decorated Olympian in history

"God's vantage point is so far above ours. He doesn't just look at the present. He sees way beyond the tomorrow. Jeff and Becki believed in the perfect plan God had for their son and trusted that Johnny's disability would inspire and challenge so many people. Romans 8:28 comes to mind as a display of God's sovereignty through Johnny's story. If we walk by faith and remember that God is greater than any obstacle we face, He can help us all overcome our own impossible mile. I was encouraged by Johnny's story, and I hope you will be, too."

—Tim Tebow, NFL player, *New York Times* best-selling author, and winner of the Heisman Trophy

"Johnny Agar's life is a story of perseverance and showing that you can accomplish anything with will and determination. More than anything, he has proven throughout his life that you can come through when you need to come through, no matter what life throws at you."

—Tom Izzo, head coach for men's basketball at Michigan State University Spartans

"Reading *The Impossible Mile* has impacted my thought process regarding my approach to coaching. It has renewed my spirit and drive, and I want to use Johnny's story as a platform to facilitate teamwork and perseverance in my coaching."

—Patrick Sullivan, director of recruitment for men's basketball at the University of North Carolina Tar Heels

"When Johnny participated in DATEV Challenge Roth in Roth, Germany . . . he helped transform the way people view those with disabilities. When we overheard a young girl look up to her mother and say, 'I didn't know people in wheelchairs could be athletes!' we knew Johnny's participation was going to change lives. We can only imagine how *The Impossible Mile* will impact many more toward a positive change."

—Zibi Szlufcik, president of the board
for Challenge Family triathlons

"*The Impossible Mile* is a compelling testimony to the power a positive attitude has on achieving the goals you set out for yourself."

—Dave Haffner, former CEO and chair of Leggett & Platt

"*The Impossible Mile* is a gift to all of us because it reminds us that no dream is ever out of reach. With so many people saying you can't, Johnny Agar said, 'I will!'"

—Jim "the Rookie" Morris, relief pitcher for the
Tampa Bay Devil Rays, inspiration behind Disney's
The Rookie, author of *The Rookie and Dream Makers*

"Johnny Agar is a true testament to what Ironman represents—defying the odds and proving that 'Anything is Possible' with each step he takes! Johnny displays determination and courage, and his story is an inspirational example to never lose sight of your personal finish line."

—Andrew Messick, president and chief
executive officer for The Ironman Group

"Upon receiving the John F. Kennedy Profile in Courage Award, my dad remarked, 'The greatest defeat of all would be to live without courage, for that would hardly be living at all.' This book was a great reminder for us all to take that courageous first step. When the goal seems overwhelming, it is the strength of the human spirit, our determination, and our resilience that propel us forward. Johnny Agar is proof of that!"

—Michael Ford, son of President Gerald
R. Ford and Mrs. Betty Ford

THE IMPOSSIBLE MILE

THE POWER IN LIVING LIFE ONE STEP AT A TIME

JOHNNY AGAR

WITH BECKI AGAR

DEXTERITY
NASHVILLE

Dexterity, LLC
604 Magnolia Lane
Nashville, TN 37211

Printed in the United States of America.

First edition: 2021
10 9 8 7 6 5 4 3 2 1

ISBN: 978-1-947297-37-1 (Hard cover)
ISBN: 978-1-947297-38-8 (eBook)
ISBN: 978-1-947297-39-5 (Audiobook)

Publisher's Cataloging-in-Publication data

Names: Agar, Johnny, author. | Agar, Becki, author.
Title: The impossible mile : the power in living life one step at a time / by Johnny
Agar, with Becki Agar.
Description: Nashville, TN: Dexterity, 2021.
Identifiers: ISBN: 978-1-947297-37-1 (hardcover) | 978-1-947297-38-8 (ebook) |
978-1-947297-39-5 (audio)
Subjects: LCSH Agar, Johnny. | Athletes—Biography. | People with disabilities—
United States—Biography. | Sports for people with disabilities. | Athletes with
disabilities. | Christian biography. | BISAC RELIGION / Christian Living /
Personal Memoirs | BIOGRAPHY & AUTOBIOGRAPHY / Sports | SELF-HELP /
Motivational & Inspirational
Classification: LCC GV697 .A43 2021 | DDC 796/.092–dc23

Book design by PerfecType, Nashville, TN.
Cover design by The Brain Design.

The authors are represented by Tom Dean, Founder & Literary Agent with A Drop of
Ink LLC, www.adropofink.pub

DEDICATION

(Johnny) *To all those who are afraid to
walk their impossible mile—
There's something deep inside you that wants to
be set free. Don't be afraid to let it go.
It's called determination.*

(Becki) *To my husband, no mile seems
impossible with you beside me.*

TABLE OF CONTENTS

Foreword by Scott Van Pelt   ix

PART I: THE ROAD TO LEARNING

Chapter 1: The Idea   3
Chapter 2: Choices   11
Chapter 3: Love Rocks   35
Chapter 4: Taking Flight   47
Chapter 5: Toolbox   71
Chapter 6: Best Friends   89

PART II: THE ROAD TO DOING

Chapter 7: First Taste   111
Chapter 8: The Beacon   125
Chapter 9: Framework   141
Chapter 10: Walk of Faith   157

PART III: THE ROAD TO ACHIEVING

Chapter 11: The Successful Failure   181
Chapter 12: Dreamer   201
Chapter 13: Will Finds a Way   217
Chapter 14: Ready to Live   237

Acknowledgments   245
Publishing Acknowledgments   257
About the Authors   259

FOREWORD

We aren't supposed to root in this business, but we all do. We have our allegiances. The teams we grew up with, the players whose posters hung on our walls. Our favorites. I met an athlete who I have no problem telling you instantly became a favorite. He's part of a team—TeamAgar—and you can say he's the star: Johnny Agar.

A few years back, at the Odyssey Theater on Under Armour's campus in Baltimore, Maryland, I met Johnny in the greenroom before an interview. His sisters, Annie and Gracy, were sitting to his left around a coffee table, Jeff, Johnny's dad, was talking to someone off to his right, and on the couch in front of him was his mom, Becki. And there in the middle of it all was Johnny in his wheelchair, smiling. It was fitting that he was surrounded by his family. A family who plays with the cards they've been dealt with great courage. It is something they have done all their lives. They are a portrait of love and support.

I immediately walked over to Johnny and introduced myself. He smiled broadly again and said, "Thank you so much for doing this. I really appreciate it!" There was something about Johnny that was just . . . more. The best compliment I can pay to anyone is that they are memorable. When you meet someone, do you think about them afterward? I couldn't stop thinking about Johnny. He has cerebral palsy, a muscle disorder that makes every movement difficult—and walking nearly impossible—but he's lived his life without limits. He is a wonderful set of contradictions, counterintuitive to what we all understand.

Johnny is humble yet hungry. Going after what he wants, but realizing he reaches his goals because of his efforts and the efforts of the team that surrounds him.

He has every reason to be bitter, yet he is so grateful. So very grateful for the people who support him, and for the chance to train and compete and to be an athlete, to be in the arena.

He is serious yet funny. When he's competing in a race and trips up because his leg crosses over the other and his feet end up in a tangled mess, Johnny is the first to joke that Olympic marathoner Meb Keflezighi never has to put up with this.

He is afraid yet brave. Johnny was never given anything easily. He will tell you he catches a lot of attention because he sometimes does things that are embarrassing. Like the time he was driving his chair to his class in college, cut the curve of the sidewalk too sharply, hit a ditch, and ended up lopsided on the ground with his face planted in the grass. He looked up at the pretty girl who came to help, smiled a grassy grin, and joked, "Hi! I just wanted to get a different vantage point of campus from down here!"

Those uneasy moments have a tendency to make people retreat to avoid the looks. But not Johnny. To know Johnny is to see an example of courage and grace in someone who shows what it means to be brave. Not to be unafraid, but to stare a challenge in the eye and step toward it, rather than away from it.

Johnny helps me recalibrate what I think adversity looks like. He grounds me in what matters and what it means to tackle a challenge. He impacts me, leaves a mark that isn't going away. Just spending time in his orbit was special—perspective and all that, right? Makes me grateful.

I know Johnny already has a team of five. You could say his team's already on the floor. But I'll be rooting for him, wherever, whenever.

And I know after reading his story, you will be rooting for him, too. I'll save you a spot on his team's bench right next to me.

—Scott Van Pelt, *SportsCenter* anchor at ESPN

PART I

The Road to Learning

CHAPTER 1

[The Idea]

Of course I knew I was different.

I took stock of my eighteen-year-old body. Most of the time my legs stuck straight out, like I didn't have functional knees, and every now and then they'd absolutely shake, as if they were taut rubber bands someone had just snapped. My feet would turn a dark purply color when I sat for long periods. And when I was cold—which was pretty often—they'd turn even darker.

My right arm was perpetually bent at a forty-five-degree angle. I couldn't turn my hands over to see my palms. Imagine *never* being able to see your own palms! And three of my fingers liked to bend upward at the knuckle, instead of curling down.

Whenever I was tired, my left eye would casually float away like a balloon. The only way to call it back was to cover my right eye, which forced my left eye to focus back where it needed to be.

My brain would tell my body to do one thing, but my body would go rogue. "Sit up," my brain would say, to which my body would respond by falling over sideways. Because of this constant war, my response time to almost anything was delayed by a few seconds. An action, a question, a task . . . whatever it was, I was slower than everyone I knew.

But inside of me? I had the exact same desires and aspirations as the next guy. If anyone looked past my body, they'd see that I wanted the same things they did. I wanted friends who made me laugh and friends *I* could make laugh. To hold a girl's hand. To love and be loved. A promising future and to live without regrets.

So maybe I was different, but I was also a typical kid. I just happened to have cerebral palsy.

THE INVITATION

When I was growing up, if you'd asked me what I aspired to be, my answer would've been automatic. *Athlete.*

Maybe it was because it seemed so far out of reach, but I wanted it even more, like a child looking at a cookie jar that's too high on the shelf.

My dad, Jeff, knew this. He had been an athlete all his life and pitched for the Detroit Tigers in the minor leagues from 1985 to 1988. He knew how much I loved hearing stories about his glory days playing baseball, basketball, and football. He knew how much I loved watching games on TV, listening to them on the radio, and traipsing out to the softball fields to watch my sisters play. He knew that a game meant more to me than just a score and that athletes stood for something more than just a high salary.

That's why—when he saw an opportunity to help me—instead of giving me one cookie, he handed me the whole jar.

"Johnny," he had said when I was sixteen years old, "I'd like some company when I go running. You wanna join me?"

And just like that, he invited me into his world.

My dad was *not* a runner. He'd played professional baseball because he could throw hard and was determined, not because he could run far or fast. In fact, he'd always hated running. But he loved me, and he knew I needed to be out there with him. With other athletes.

So, he started pushing me in small races. Using an old jogging stroller that he reinforced with duct tape to hold my weight, Dad took me out almost every weekend to run in 5Ks around my hometown of Rockford, Michigan. The Buck Creek Run, the Kilt Klassic, the Irish Jig, the Lowell Pink Arrow . . . the names didn't matter, as long as we were out there together. Every race was an opportunity for me to experience life as an active participant. Dad was teaching me how to live like an athlete.

"Remember, Johnny, we can't take off too fast," he said on one starting line. "We have to pace ourselves." *Pace ourselves. Got it.*

Then later, when I heard his footsteps falling heavier, I called back to him, "How ya feeling, Dad?"

"Tired, Buddy. But we're gonna make it," he answered, breathing hard between phrases. "To that mailbox. At the corner. See it up there?" *I see it and understand. Keep pushing.*

While running wasn't foreign to Dad, running while *pushing me* was. He was forced to learn a whole new set of body mechanics. Unlike almost every other runner, he could no longer swing his arms to help maintain a rhythm and propel himself forward. Instead his hands gripped the jogger handle as he guided me down a yet-to-be discovered road.

When we ran, I felt the bumps of the pavement beneath me. I watched other runners pass us, heard their encouraging words. I learned from the pressure of the jogger on my body to tell how steep of an incline we were going up or down. I loved the feeling of the wind on my face, taking my breath away.

And it was all because of Dad. Running wasn't easy for him under ordinary circumstances. Now he was pushing an extra one hundred pounds without the benefit of his arms, and for what? Why was he putting himself through that?

I knew it was because he wanted me to see what was on the other side. To give his son a chance at understanding something intangible—a feeling, really—and I loved him all the more for it.

Dad was treating me like his teammate, and I soaked up every moment like a sponge absorbs water. At eighteen years old, I needed athletics almost as much as I needed to breathe. Running with Dad made me feel alive. It gave me a purpose—something to look forward to and strive for. I had always *read* about athletes, but actually training and running with one gave me a whole new perspective. It was magical. Gauging the sound of Dad's breathing behind me . . . deciding whether he was pacing himself properly . . . mingling with other runners . . . I was *in* their world. I had a backstage pass to the life of an athlete.

And I knew Dad wasn't running for the enjoyment of it.

He was running for me.

COMING ALIVE

Mom and Dad had always taught me that my future did not have to depend on my current situation—that I could decide what course my life would take as long as I had faith in God, worked hard, and never gave up. "If you want to look at yourself as having a disability," Dad liked to say, "then that's how people will see you, and that's how you'll live your life. Disabled. But if you really want to make a mark on this world, you need to see yourself as a champion—and that's what you'll be."

Occasionally, we ran into some of Dad's old baseball teammates, and they told me stories about how Dad was always practicing or trying to improve his game. Dan "Peaches" Petry, who pitched for the Detroit Tigers 1984 World Series team, once told me about an injury that put him on the disabled list. He rehabbed in Lakeland, Florida, at the High-A-ball minor league affiliate where Dad was playing. "Your dad was one of the hardest working players on that whole team," he told me, "partly because he was *always* asking questions to help him develop into a better player."

I loved stories like that. They confirmed what I already knew about my father. I witnessed him live like that all the time, but it was always good to hear his old friends color in the picture.

Dad taught me to persevere. He showed me how to never give up on your dreams no matter how foolish they seem, even if the odds aren't in your favor. At the same time, he taught me to be grateful. He never took playing baseball or being with the Detroit Tigers for granted. He knew he was blessed to be there and worked hard to prove it. To him, being able to do what he loved every day was a gift, and he appreciated every moment of it.

"Johnny, before I made the next level in every sport, I was *always* told I was just not good enough to make it further," he once told me. "But I used that as motivation to prove them wrong. It makes you appreciate it more when you make it—and you can do the same thing. Just because you can't move your body the way you want doesn't mean you can't push yourself to do better."

I think that's why Dad knew I needed to be an athlete. To participate in something that made me feel alive. I had lived within the confines of my rigid, tight, and tangled body for the past eighteen years. It was time for an escape. Before Dad introduced me to running, it felt like I had been sitting in a movie theater watching my family and friends act out their scenes in the movie of my life—and the only thing I could do was sit there and watch the big screen as life passed me by.

After we started running, though? I auditioned for—and *got*—a part in the movie of my life. And not only was I in the film, but I was a lot more than some random extra. Thanks to Dad, I had a supporting role with substantial lines and appearances in almost every scene.

THE IDEA

When a person's foot falls asleep, it feels like it's out of place—like it doesn't belong to their leg anymore. It's disorienting.

That's what having cerebral palsy feels like, except it feels that way throughout my whole body.

Because my mind is constantly battling my muscles, it feels like my body doesn't truly belong to me. It feels like I'm trying to operate a complicated machine with unwieldy controls and an instruction manual written in the *Game of Thrones* language Dothraki.

Running with Dad made me see something: I could rewrite *part* of that manual at least, using a language I could understand. I could take some control over the machine.

See, the fact hadn't escaped me that it was *Dad* who was putting in the hard work to train for these races. More importantly, I knew he was doing it for me. And because I looked up to him so much—as a man and as an athlete—I wanted to show him *I* could do it too. To show him how well he had taught me.

I wanted to push my body to the extreme. To know what it felt like to be so exhausted that you thought you couldn't go any farther, but then you keep going. To push yourself beyond what you think is reasonable, all because you have a goal in mind, and you want to reach it. I had watched Dad do that for me numerous times. I had seen athletes with arms in the air, fist pumping to the heavens, triumphant because they had achieved the dream they had worked so hard to attain.

I wanted that feeling. Desperately.

Except up to that point, I had only walked twenty-three steps in my life—and that was using my walker in therapy. But what if I competed in my *own* race? I could give Dad a little break, and it would be my way of thanking him for all he had done for me.

What would that look like? Simple: I'd walk the last mile in my church's annual 5K race. The idea seemed straightforward, but it was about to change my life forever.

CHAPTER 2

[Choices]

W e need to take him now."

Those were the first words the doctors said to my parents as I came into this world. It was in Beaumont Hospital at 6:04 p.m. on March 18, 1994. Knowing that I was eleven weeks early, my parents had been briefed on what to expect when I arrived. High-risk pregnancy doctors explained that the duration of pregnancies should be at least thirty-two to thirty-four weeks, and since my mom was at twenty-nine weeks with me, there were all sorts of risks involved—retinopathy, hemorrhaging, pneumonia, intestinal issues, anemia. The list was extensive.

My parents always told me that while they were concerned about all of the potential complications, their excitement for my birth far surpassed their worry. Maybe it was because I was their firstborn, or maybe it was because they were naive. Maybe it was both. But whatever the case, it was a story that set the stage for my life. They loved me no matter the outcome.

There were a lot of uncertainties in life, but if there was one thing my parents were sure of, it was their faith in God—that He had a plan for them and, now, for the three of us. They had relied on their faith throughout their seven years together, and they also relied on it throughout the pregnancy, the preterm labor, and the birth. When worry engulfed them, they leaned on their understanding of a greater plan in the works. Mom and Dad repeatedly said they would love their child no matter what, and they were not about to deviate from that now.

I spent three months in the neonatal intensive care unit. Dad would drop my mom, Becki, off at the hospital in the morning, and she would stay there with me all day, every day. Dad then joined us after work, and they both stayed with me until ten or eleven at night—sometimes later, depending on how well my day went. They spent the night over at Pa's house—I gave that name to my mom's dad, Marty Inman—since he lived only five minutes from the hospital. That meant they could be there for me at a moment's notice. Apparently, I kept the nursing staff on their toes with all of the up-and-down moments. It was not something new for them, but it was definitely unfamiliar territory for my parents. Mom and Dad could touch me in the incubator only after scrubbing their hands for three minutes with an antiseptic cleanser.

Since mom stayed with me all day, her hands cracked so badly from the constant scrubbing that anytime she bent her fingers, the tightening of the skin made them bleed. When she got back to my pa's at night, she bathed them in lotion, only to have it happen all over again the next day.

The NICU taught them both a lot, but the biggest lesson they learned was that life held no guarantees.

Every day for me was a new day of hope, of potential progress, and another day closer to going home. At first my parents told me they worried a lot. There were so many unknowns, so many things that could go wrong. They relied on so many others—doctors, nurses, and specialists—that it was overwhelming at times, but they remained faithful in God's plan.

One of the routine procedures the hospital did for all premature babies was an ultrasound of the head. They do this to make sure there are no signs of trauma, since the babies' brains are so fragile. My ultrasound came out looking a little different. It didn't look "normal." That wouldn't be the last time my parents heard that word.

The ultrasound showed a bleed in my brain, and about one week after my birth, the doctor informed my parents that I had cerebral palsy.

From that point on, they chose to raise me as though I didn't have a disability. It wasn't because they were in denial—as some of the medical community had thought—it was because they didn't want to pigeonhole me. They didn't want anything to have the potential of slowing me down in achieving what I wanted out of life. And cerebral palsy had a lot of negative expectations.

MOM & DAD

My parents chose to live their lives looking at the positives, rather than focusing on the negatives—even though Mom had every excuse to be pessimistic. Growing up in Berkley, Michigan, she had one sibling, Bret, who was four years older. They were very close. In February 1982, he died in an unexpected accident at the age of nineteen. Mom was devastated.

Four years later, Mom and her family went on vacation in the Bahamas. She and her mother, Ann, crossed the street to get to a restaurant for dinner, and while my pa paid the cab fare, my grandma was struck by an oncoming vehicle. Several days later, my mom watched her die. That left two in her family—my mom and my pa. Needless to say, family means everything to Mom. It was because of her experiences that she taught me to be grateful for both the good and the bad in my life. "God's plans are bigger than mine," she always says. That's one of the reasons why I look at my cerebral palsy as a blessing.

In his family, Dad has two siblings: John, who is two years older, and Kathy, who is four years younger. They were raised in Portage, Michigan. All the kids were involved in some sport year-round, and when there was no sport in season, they would throw baseballs against a wire fence or shoot baskets on the small homemade half-court they had in their backyard. For Dad, every summer involved working part time while training and playing baseball in various leagues. When he got the call in 1984 to join the Detroit Tigers' minor league organization, the year they won the World Series, the whole family had a party to celebrate his hard work.

Dad says he had a great childhood. His family didn't have a lot of money, and his parents, Jerry and Mary Ellen Agar, struggled in their marriage, but he considered himself fortunate to have grown up in a household where he was always encouraged, where laughter was always present, and where he knew his family always had his back. He was steadfast in reaching his goals and did it through hard work and perseverance. When I was born, he said it was his mission to ensure I had the same opportunities—or better—to become successful in whatever I worked hard for. Regardless of whether or not I had a disability.

Mom and Dad have always said it was providence that brought them together. I would have to agree, since they turned out to be the perfect mix for what I was going to need in life. Both were raised to value hard work, perseverance, love for one another, and a strong faith. Through a series of "God-incidences," as Mom calls them, they both chose the same college—Grand Valley State University, a small university in western Michigan. Mom was studying sociology and psychology, while Dad was "studying" my mom, he likes to say. Actually, during the off-season of baseball, he would go back to school to earn his degree in computer science. He eventually got a master's degree in finance from Michigan State University. He had a unique ability to follow his dreams and also be realistic in his approach to them.

They met one night at a house party on campus in 1985 and talked for forty-five minutes about what they were studying, how they ended up at Grand Valley, and friends they had in common. Dad noticed that Mom was shivering from the cold and offered her his Detroit Tigers jacket. He was trying to impress her.

The next day, as the story goes, Dad saw Mom walking in one of the study halls. She said hi to him by name, and he responded, "Hi, um, what was your name again?" It was a blow to her ego, but according to Mom he made up for it a hundredfold after that mistake.

Dad constantly wooed Mom with surprise picnic dates to the lake and occasionally showed up at one of her classes to hand the professor a single red rose to give to her. The professor, unsure of who should receive the rose, would ask Dad for clarity. "She's the most beautiful brunette in your class," he would reply. The roses were usually given out on the anniversary of her brother's death to show he was thinking of her.

When my grandma died suddenly in 1986, Mom and Dad had been dating for about six months. Dad was in the middle of spring training in Florida, trying to make the cut for the season, when he got the call from Mom that her mom had passed away. His heart broke for her, and he became angry that he was not there to support her.

Mom, Pa, and my mom's maternal grandparents flew back from the Bahamas with Grandma Ann's remains on a US Air

Force plane. A senator from Michigan sent the plane as an act of goodwill. As they taxied to the tarmac, Mom said she looked out the window, and there standing with his arms crossed and legs slightly parted like a "superhero without a cape," she says, was Dad waiting for her. He had chosen to risk losing his shot at playing baseball—something he had worked hard for since he was a little boy—for her. She said she knew at that moment she would marry him.

Apparently Dad had the same thought. At a football game at Grand Valley the next year—and in front of my mom's family and my dad's mom and sister—Dad's friends unrolled a huge banner on the field during a time-out. It read, "Becki, will you marry me?" My mom looked to her right, and my dad was there holding a box with a ring in it. Everyone in the stadium stopped what they were doing, even the players on the field, as they waited for Mom's resounding "Yes!"

EARLY DAYS

When Dad played baseball in the minors, he threw extremely hard with pitches clocked in the low nineties. His career started in 1985 with the Gastonia Jets, a Low-A-level team in North Carolina for the Tigers. From there he went to Lakeland and then moved up to the Glens Falls Tigers (Double-A) in New York. Mom visited him on her spring breaks from college. Dad showed her around the town in the morning, and by early afternoon he had to report to the stadium for that evening's game. Afterward, Dad took Mom out for dinner, or they hung out with some of the other players and their girlfriends.

Mom told me one time that Dad called to tell her he had gotten selected to pitch for the Triple-A Toledo Mud Hens in a game against the Detroit Tigers. He wondered if she would like to drive to Ohio to watch him pitch. She didn't hesitate. From the stands on that hot summer day, Mom said she could see some of the Tiger greats—Petry, Jack Morris, Lance Parrish, Dave Bergman, and Kirk Gibson—and there, on the same field, was her fiancé.

Mom attended as many games as possible. She sat behind home plate and waited for Dad to come into the game at the most critical time, since he was a reliever. Mom loved the energy in the stadium. The fans at minor league games are some of the best because they truly love baseball. After games they lined up outside the locker room to get autographs from the players who might make it to the "bigs."

My parents said they relished their time together before Mom had to go back to college. It would be a year later when they became husband and wife—and cross-country good-byes became obsolete.

HOME

My parents' first house as a married couple was in a neighborhood that was tucked in between the busy thoroughfares of Livonia,

Michigan, almost as if it were protected by the reality of what was happening outside our little world. Every road out of our subdivision led to the hustle and bustle of the city, but inside our little neighborhood, it was quiet, safe, and warm—like a home should be. It was the perfect place to start a family, which is exactly why my parents had chosen it.

Mom said when word got out to their next-door neighbor Larry that Dad had once played with the Detroit Tigers, he started coming over with his ball and glove to have a catch and talk baseball. A huge fan of the game, he was elated to brag to people at work the next day about playing catch with a Tigers pitcher.

Outside their front door, Larry would stand there tossing the ball in his glove and asking if Dad could "throw a few" to him. Dad said he loved playing catch with people, but he never threw hard to anyone because they usually had no idea how much it would hurt. For the first pitch, he went easy on Larry to see if he could even catch the ball. He caught it—and was in immediate pain. Larry stood up right away, throwing his glove on the ground and shaking his hand violently. Dad was glad he hadn't thrown him his fastball. Mom said Larry's swollen hand was a badge of honor.

Loving their life together, Mom and Dad knew something was missing to make their house truly a home—and that something was a child. Not two years into living there, Mom became pregnant with me. They had been trying for a little while, so when Mom had an inkling she was pregnant, she waited for Dad to leave for work and then ran upstairs to take a pregnancy test. She had prayed for a baby to be growing inside her belly. She had prayed for me.

What they didn't plan on were the complications that came with my birth. The unknowns and the what-ifs of raising a child with cerebral palsy. And while they were scared, they knew they had their faith and their determination to strengthen them along the way. They loved me unconditionally and knew I would be loved by the rest of my family, who would help in showing me how to succeed in life.

THE TOWEL TEST

I was about four months old when my mother started seeing things about me that did not seem right. She noticed I was having a hard time holding up my head. It seemed to stay up for a second and then quickly flop back down, sometimes causing me to cry because my head had hit either the floor, mattress, or Mom's shoulder so hard. She never remembered holding a baby and having its head flop down continually like mine. It was her first indication of my cerebral palsy diagnosis just months before.

She started to notice other things too. My right hand stayed clenched a lot of the time, my body stiffened when I got excited, I barely cooed or made sounds, I was not reaching for toys, and I couldn't track something moving in front of me.

When my parents received my diagnosis, the doctor had also told them he was unsure of my cognitive abilities. Because of this, my parents were concerned I wouldn't be aware of the world around me. Based on my behaviors, Mom decided to call the pediatrician to voice her concerns. The pediatrician told her to try the towel test. She wanted Mom to put a small towel over my face. If I showed displeasure with having it on my face or reached to take it off, that would be a good sign.

All day long she had debated with herself whether or not she should put something over my face. *Would it make a difference, really?* She knew she wasn't going to treat me any differently than she did already. She also didn't tell Dad, because telling him made the situation more real.

She told me that she tried putting it out of her head, but by the next morning the need to know was gnawing away at her. She went to put a bottle in the fridge, and when she brushed her hip up against the oven door, a small dish towel fell to the floor— almost taunting her for being such a coward. Never wanting to be thought of as a coward, Mom said she went and picked me up out of my bouncer seat and laid me on the kitchen floor. Dad had gone to work, so it was just her and me.

She said she looked at me, so happy that morning, and as my stiff body tried to make happy movements, she placed the dish towel gently over my face.

And I did nothing.

Mom said she quickly pulled it off and began to cry. "Stupid towel test," she said to me as I laid on the kitchen floor. She then picked me up and held me close with her head resting on the top of mine. She said she felt ashamed because she knew she didn't need to do a towel test to know that it didn't matter what response I had; she was still going to love me unequivocally.

RESOLVE

Up to this point, life was running smoothly for us. It was easy to deal with their choice of raising me as though I had no disability, because it had been just the three of us, and we were surrounded by a loving family who was excited to see their grandchild or nephew every time we visited. Mom and Dad were having fun watching me grow, learning how to become parents, getting a feel for what my likes and dislikes were. And when I wasn't sleeping, we were enjoying the summer, with walks outside almost every day or night. However, their resolve would be tested soon.

My parents were anxious to begin the early intervention program for me to receive therapy. They were excited to bring in professionals who would be better able to help me. Since I was still so young at six months old, the physical and occupational therapists would come to our home for forty-five minutes to an hour each visit.

By September, my first appointment had been lined up with a physical therapist. Mom said she had been so nervous. She cleaned the house, put some coffee on, and played some Debussy in the background. She said she loved playing soft classical music or soft classics, especially at night when she was getting me ready for my bath. She would set out my pajamas and towel so they were ready for me when I got out of the blue tub that fit in our kitchen sink. After my bath, she would carry me over to our big, plump couch, sit down, cradle me in her arms, and feed me until I fell asleep to her humming "Into the Mystic" by Van Morrison or "Annie's Theme" from the *Father of the Bride* soundtrack. The music and the routine of the evening had a calming effect on her.

So, it was no surprise when she told me she turned on the music softly for this first meeting with the therapist. She had been anxious. So many questions went through her head. *Would the physical therapist be disappointed in my progress? Would she find something wrong with me that the doctors didn't catch? Would I like her? Would she like me?* She said just as she was going over all those questions in her head, the doorbell rang.

That moment, Mom told me, she wasn't only opening the door to let the therapist in, but she was also opening the door to a new reality. She had opened the floodgates of opinion, judgment, and criticism, and found out exactly what it was going to mean to live with courage in their convictions.

The therapist's name was Stacy, and she asked if they could sit at the kitchen table to talk and fill out paperwork. To make room, Mom moved a bowl filled with cauliflower, broccoli, and carrots that she had crafted out of crepe paper and Styrofoam. She was so proud when people couldn't believe she had made them, but now she said she couldn't help feeling they were inadequate, because that's how she felt at the moment.

Stacy pulled out a small file folder full of papers. Years later, when Mom was recalling the story, she detailed the conversation they had.

"I see you had called back in August with a therapy request," Stacy said. "How did you hear about us?"

Mom said it had been my pediatrician who had told us about the therapy center.

Stacy wrote something down and replied, "Well, it's really good that you scheduled to have John be seen at six months. I love it when parents get their kids in as soon as possible."

As a song by Rachmaninoff began to play in the background, the therapist continued, "Great. Okay, let's see. Johnny was born eleven weeks early, is that right?"

"Yes, it is."

"And it says that you had a normal pregnancy. No trauma, like car accidents or falls?"

"No. I had a great pregnancy. We think Johnny was just ready to see the world a little sooner than we thought," Mom said. She smiled a little to try to make the situation more of a relaxed one for her, but the therapist didn't catch on to her attempt.

Stacy looked at her checklist. "He weighed three pounds, seven ounces? Wow, he was a big baby for a twenty-nine-weeker!"

"Yes, I guess so," Mom answered. "He was much bigger than most of the babies in the NICU is all I know!" She smiled big and proud.

Reading another document, Stacy said, "Okay, it also says he was on the vent for less than twenty-four hours. That's good! However, they found a bleed in his brain that led to his diagnosis of spastic quadriplegia cerebral palsy."

Mom said she felt like she was going to be sick. She had a feeling that what she was going to say next was not going to go over well. Processing her thoughts, she softly said to Stacy, "Could you do me a favor? My husband and I have decided that we are not going to mention cerebral palsy around Johnny at all until he is old enough to understand it himself. We don't want to place any limits on him. So could you please not say anything about his diagnosis when he's around?"

Stacy gave a smile that appeared to be more condescending than sympathetic. Mom said although she had been a new parent, she wasn't oblivious about the implication of that look, whether Stacy intended it or not.

"I'm not sure I understand?" Stacy said. "He is going to know that he will have limitations because he will not be able to do things like the other kids his age can." She did not mean for it to sound so rude. To her, she was just stating a fact and not seeing the ramifications her words could have on me, who now sat in Mom's lap.

Mom said she felt awkward, embarrassed, but more determined than ever to remain steadfast in what she and my dad had decided about the course of my life. She also said it was her first taste of what was to come.

"We just want to treat him as our son," Mom said, stumbling over words while holding back tears.

"I know this has been hard for you," Stacy said, reaching out to touch Mom's hand, "but you will probably understand and get a better picture as time goes on."

Mom said she was crushed. She now had a good idea of what they were up against raising me, a special-needs child, as though I didn't have special needs.

Stacy and another therapist continued to work with me in our home once a week, and my parents worked with me nonstop. Both therapists agreed to Mom and Dad's terms of not mentioning that I had cerebral palsy. Mom thought they got together at times to have a good laugh about "the Agar family and their strange request" because the therapists independently said the same canned thing to her: "Just remember, he will wonder why he can't do things and you eventually are going to have to tell him."

"TYPICAL"

For two years, Mom and Dad said I was still unable to sit up, say anything, or walk. But while I couldn't do a lot physically, they said I was developing my own personality. My face became very animated when my parents spoke to me. I was responding to what they were saying even if I didn't do it in the usual fashion for a child of two years. I smiled and made these high-pitched noises when I got excited about something. While my upper body remained as stiff as a board, my legs kicked like crazy, and my face lit up. They said I clearly knew the world around me. *Stupid towel test.*

They said my emotive face made me appear to the average person like I didn't have cerebral palsy at all. This proved to be a challenge in public. At the grocery store, at the mall, at restaurants, in the park, in the library, everywhere we went, my parents said it seemed like people noticed the cute little baby in the stroller, but when they stopped to ooh and aah, my rigid body went into action and I started to smile and kick my legs at them to give them my version of "hi." When they noticed my differences, inevitably, Dad said they would look at Mom and him and say, "Oh, I'm so sorry. I thought he was a normal little boy," or, "Oh, is that normal for him to do that?"

So my parents chose to ban the word "normal" from their vocabulary. "What is normal anyway?" they asked. They didn't want me to hear that when I wasn't old enough to understand and assume I must be abnormal. It had a negative connotation they wanted to avoid. From then on, they agreed to replace the word "normal" with "typical."

Mom and Dad said they armed themselves when they took me out in public, and they were always on guard. Still, sometimes the comments from others cut right to their heart—especially early on when they were still new parents and vulnerable to the opinions of others. They told me a story about going to Mass on Christmas Eve when I was two years old.

The church was packed, and people were squeezed tightly into the pews. It was a bitter cold evening that night, and everyone had been bundled up. When they sat down and settled in, however, it became quite warm. Winter coats were shed, which made the pews even more cramped. I was sitting on Mom's lap, and Dad sat next to us. On the other side of her was a man with his young daughter on his lap.

Mom said she was trying to get me situated into a comfortable position when, ironically, during the absolution of the Mass when the priest says, "May Almighty God have mercy on us, forgive us our sins, and bring us to eternal life," the man sitting next to her leaned over and asked with a whisper, "Is what he has contagious? Because I don't want my little girl to get it."

Mom said she was stunned and quickly responded, "No." She said tears began to well in her eyes, and she began to tremble. Her movement caught the attention of Dad, and he asked if everything was all right. She couldn't speak for fear of losing all of her faculties right there in the middle of Christmas Eve Mass and saying something she would regret. She said she held onto me tightly and looked up at the huge crucifix and prayed for my future. Mom also prayed for the man who had no clue how hurtful his words had been.

THE SMALL THINGS

Fortunately for me, my parents continued to stay the course in raising me with the idea of no limits. I was extremely slow at hitting any physical milestones by the "chart standard," but my parents still rejoiced in the small things. No movement or expression I made was ever taken for granted, they said. There were so many unknowns with me that everything I did was a momentous reason for joy.

One time on a sunny afternoon at the start of spring, Mom had me on the floor in the family room playing. I had just turned two, and I was getting over a cold. Dad was in his office getting some work done, and we were busy having fun. Then it happened. I reached up with my left hand and I picked my nose. You would have thought I walked on the moon! Mom excitedly hollered for Dad to come out and watch me pick my nose. She called all the family members to tell them the good news as well. "Johnny picked his nose!" she would say. I can just imagine their faces on the other side of the phone. But to my parents, that was a huge step. I was able to separate my one finger and with a controlled, skillful movement direct it toward my tiny little nostril. Like I said, they rejoiced at every tiny accomplishment—and picking my nose was no exception.

GROWING OUR FAMILY

Mom and Dad wanted to fill their home with more children, so it was no surprise to everyone when they announced Mom was pregnant with a second child. Actually, I made the announcement to everyone with a shirt that read "I'm going to be a big brother."

My sister Breann was born in April 1996, one month after I turned two years old. They were going to nickname her "Bree," but I couldn't say that. All I could say was the last syllable of her name and I dragged that out with my tongue to make it sound like "Annie." So that's what we called her. My parents said as soon as I met her, I was hooked. She was my baby, and I wanted her to go everywhere with me. Mom often laid us on the floor together and encouraged me to "show her how to do things." I loved to do that, and Mom loved it because she was able to sneak in a little more therapy time for me. Annie became my encourager—and still is to this day.

Since Mom had come from a small family, she had dreamed about having a lot of kids, and Dad had always said he wanted to have enough kids for a baseball team. Mom liked that idea. However, after complications from Annie's birth—where Mom developed a lung embolism from being on bed rest for most of the pregnancy—the doctors suggested she not become pregnant again. They also said to count our blessings that Mom was still here with us. Knowing that their best-laid plans may not be God's plans, my parents accepted the fact that their "baseball team" may not come about.

Still, they knew in their hearts their family was not complete. Several years later, Mom and Dad sat us down and asked us if we would like to add another sister or brother to the family. When they told us they wanted to adopt a baby, Annie and I were ecstatic and couldn't wait to add a sibling to the

Agar household. On September 28, 2002, we were blessed with a baby girl we named Grace Elizabeth. "Grace" because we believed she was a blessing to all of us and "Elizabeth" in tribute to her birthmother's sister. Gracy continually reminds me how to be strong in the face of adversity and to not give up on my dreams.

MOVING FORWARD

I started receiving therapy at a rehabilitation facility called Mary Free Bed at the age of three. It was about twenty minutes from home and was quite well known for its world-class treatment for children and adults. Three times a week, Mom put Annie and me in our car seats and head over to "play." That's what they called it.

While Annie kept busy with an assortment of toys at her disposal, the therapists stretched my muscles to loosen everything up. They concentrated on my right arm and my right hand since that side gave me the most trouble. However, just to keep things interesting, it was the opposite for my lower body: my left leg gave me more trouble. They had me do things like cross midline, support my weight, and pronate my wrist. All I knew was that it wore me out. I also knew it wasn't "play." It was hard work.

The therapists at Mary Free Bed also introduced me to my first walker—and I hated it. Using it was so much for me to think about. I eventually got to a point where I could stand in it but couldn't move my feet. Mom offered me all the things I loved—chocolate, milkshakes, more time on the computer with Dad—just to get me to try to take a step. Sometimes it worked, and sometimes it didn't.

Like most kids, my favorite character was Mickey Mouse. Mom and Dad had the idea to bribe me with a trip to Disney World to see Mickey in person. They said if I was able to take two steps, one for each foot in my walker, they would take me to see Mickey and I could tell him myself what I was able to do. In the days leading up to my next therapy session, Mom hyped up the idea by reading Disney stories, dressing me in my Buzz Lightyear pajamas, and playing with Disney characters.

Therapy day was finally here. After about forty-five minutes of working and manipulating my muscles, it was time to try the walker. While I donned a Disney sweatshirt, Mom and Annie watched on as my face winced and my body twisted and contorted trying to get my leg to move.

I recently received leg braces that covered my foot and went up to my knee. They were made of a hard, white plastic with a big, jointed knob at the ankles to provide support for my weak legs and to keep my foot positioned properly. Having these braces on made taking a step even harder. The therapist put her hands on mine as a reminder to hold on, and she gave me verbal cues too. "Hold on with both hands," "shift your weight to the left," "lean forward a bit and bend your knee to lift your foot."

After about ten minutes of struggling, with the therapist almost ready to give up, I was able to bend my right leg and take a step. My right foot immediately crossed over and landed on top of the toes of my left. "That's it, Johnny!" Mom said with tears streaming down her face. "Mickey's waiting for you! Just one more step with your other leg!" Even Annie had stopped what she was doing to look on and encourage me. "Mon, Nonny, do it!" she cheered. The therapist gently grabbed ahold of my foot and wrestled it away from the big ankle on the brace from the left side of my body and placed it back on the right side.

"Keep it going, Johnny," the therapist urged. "Do the same thing. Shift your weight now to the right side, and bend at the knee to move that left leg." After several tries, somehow without bending my knee too much, I was able to swing my left leg to the front, and I took another step. Mom swooshed me up into the air, and we danced with Annie—right there on the floor of the therapy room. Everyone stared, but we didn't care; we danced and sang anyway.

When we got back in the car and headed for home, I remember catching a glimpse of Mom in the rearview mirror and saw tears streaming down her face. She told me on the ride back how proud she was because I stuck with it when it was hard and I never gave up.

I think that's what made her the proudest. Not that I took the steps, but that she had seen in me that day the perseverance and tenacity I was going to need for the rest of my life. That I had proven to myself—and to them—that once I put my mind toward something, I could accomplish anything. She knew at that point I was going to be all right.

My parents kept good on their promise, and I told Mickey Mouse how I earned a trip to Disney World. It would be twenty years later when I would walk there again . . . in the Disney Marathon.

CHAPTER 3

[Love Rocks]

My family has always been there for me. My grandparents and aunts and uncles were so important in helping to steer me in the right direction. A direction that gave me every opportunity to succeed as much as the next guy. They respected my parents' wishes and never mentioned my disability in front of me. While the struggles I had were hard for them to watch, they listened to my parents early on and chose to make it a priority to teach me, rather than baby me. If I had difficulty reaching for something, they took my arm and encouraged me to get it myself. "C'mon Johnny, a little farther! Reach!" they said.

My dad's mother would have done anything for me. One time Mom had mentioned to her in passing how she thought this particular toy might help motivate me to crawl more. The toy was always sold out everywhere they looked, so Grandma made it her mission to find it. She had always been a doer. She called the toy manufacturer, explained why she needed it, included my short life story, and convinced the person to look up the freight schedule for the Kalamazoo, Michigan, store. On the anticipated date of arrival, Grandma was there waiting for the delivery, took four of the toys, and thanked the shocked driver . . . but apparently not before telling him all about her grandson!

Aunt Kathy, my dad's sister, and her new husband, Rick, watched Annie and me a lot of weekends at their house. With no children of their own, and no experience with kids yet, their love for us overcame their fears, and they introduced us to what adventure was all about. Every moment with them was fun and full of laughter. Aunt Kathy would make crafts with us, and Uncle Rick, a rather strong guy, would grab hold of my waist, make the noise of a plane's engine, and lift me up off of the ground, flying me around the room with my rigid arms at my sides, my body tight, and my legs kicking like crazy. For a kid who was limited in what he could do and who moved very slowly, those airplane rides were magical.

LESSON LEARNED

Pa lived only twenty minutes from us, and I got to see him almost daily. Since he was such a special part of our lives, when Dad took a new job on the other side of the state, Mom told Pa he would be moving with us. And he did. In fact, he moved into a condo on the lake right around the corner from our house. That way he could pick "Johnny Boy" up in his bass boat to go fishing all the time. Pa would come over and show me the newest fishing lure he had bought, saying he knew I would catch the biggest fish in the lake with it. He loved seeing me happy and tried his best to keep me that way. "When Johnny Boy is happy, I'm happy," he always said.

That's why it was so hard for him to see me struggle as I tried to learn how to do things on my own. I remember Pa had gotten Annie a wooden rocking chair for her second birthday. I had just turned four years old. The rocking chair was the perfect size for her to sit in and read stories to her stuffed animals. It always sat in our family room next to our big couch.

Pa was over one day, and we had just finished lunch. Mom had me crawl over to the couch, where she positioned me in between two cushions to help me sit better. I was getting pretty good at army crawling everywhere—the friction burns on my elbows from the wood floor and carpet were proof of it. Mom and Dad had me crawl to keep me moving and for some good exercise. Eventually my physical therapist gave them a small square scooter board that had wheels on it and was about two inches off the ground. We would put it on the wood floor and Dad would lay my belly on top of it so my legs and arms were hanging off. That is how we played hockey, tag, and hide-and-seek, and unfortunately for me, it's also how I completed my designated chore of cleaning the floor.

Pa sat next to me on the couch, and we started talking about what fish we were going to catch that weekend and how the Tigers were going to do in their next game. Pa told me all about one of his favorite baseball players, named Joe DiMaggio—"Joltin' Joe" they called him—and how he remembered following the hitting streak that helped Joe make his mark on baseball history. "He got a hit in fifty-six consecutive games, more than anyone else ever had before," Pa told me. Pa described how calm Joe stood at the plate, even with so much pressure on him. "He knew he might fail any time he went up to bat, but he rose to the challenge," Pa said. "That's what I want you to do, Johnny Boy. Never give up, keep on trying."

Mom was finishing up in the kitchen and kept hearing Pa say, "Johnny, you gotta sit up so Pa can see your face." My upper body always wanted to lean to the right until eventually I fell over. We constantly worked on keeping my hands down to support my weight, but inevitably my hands crept back up to my ears—especially when I got excited talking about things like catching fish and Tigers baseball.

Mom came over, took a look at me falling over for about the seventh time, and had a thought for a better seating position.

"Johnny," she said, "I have an idea. Why don't you sit on Annie's rocking chair? That way Pa can sit right next to you on the couch, and you can hold onto the arms of the chair to keep you upright." Theoretically it was a great idea, until we tried it. The movement of the chair, along with having to hold myself up, freaked me out. I immediately arched my back to get down and began to scream in fear.

"That's all right," Pa said. "He can just sit next to me on the couch, and I will push him up when he needs it. I'm sure he won't fall over again. Right, Johnny Boy?"

I didn't respond to my grandpa's question. My focus was on getting out of that chair. Mom was kneeling on the floor next to the chair and set me on her lap. She calmed me down so she could talk to me.

"Johnny, what are you not liking about this chair? Are you afraid that you are going to fall?"

My red, tear-soaked face nodded yes.

"Do you think Pa or I would let you fall? We don't want you to hurt yourself either, so we're gonna make sure you're stable in that chair, okay?"

I still wanted nothing to do with it. Little Annie came over, attempted to wipe the tears off my face, and said, "It's all right, Nonny, see?" She jumped over and sat down in her rocking chair to show me how it's done.

If there was one thing my parents wanted for me, it was to show me I could do anything, even if I was afraid to try. This rocking chair wasn't going to win the battle; Mom wanted to make sure I won. Over and over again she sat me in that chair, and over and over again I cried, arched my back, and threw my hands up to my ears.

Annie left the room.

Pa had tears in his eyes watching me struggle with what I knew I could do but didn't want to because I was scared.

The harder I resisted, the harder Mom pushed me toward my fear. After about forty-five minutes of assuring me through her words, hugs, and encouragement, I finally sat down. With Mom's help, I was able to place my hands down on the arms of the chair. I took a deep, jerky breath to gain my composure, looked up at Pa, and said, "Will you stay and watch the Tigers with me?"

He answered, "Anything for you, Johnny Boy."

I hated that rocking chair, but had I not conquered my fear of it, I would have never known what I was capable of. Mom knew that, and she knew I needed to know it too.

I always thought about that rocking chair when I had to face my fears in other situations. Experiences like that—along with the guidance my family continually gave me—helped to shape me as I was growing up.

NATURE CALLS

When I had to start kindergarten, I was really nervous. So many unknowns. It was difficult just getting to my classroom. I was always tardy because I had to take the elevator. Once I got settled, I struggled to participate because of the delay in my movements; it was impossible for me to raise my hand quickly enough to answer questions. There just wasn't enough time for the teachers to wait on me, even though they tried. I became very quiet and withdrawn.

My parents also wanted me to have time for fun things. There were just not enough hours in the day for all of the extracurricular activities I wanted to do. School took seven to eight hours, and then I had speech, occupational, and physical therapies every week. I was literally falling asleep at the dinner table. That's when they chose to homeschool me. It would free up more time for us to include some fun things into our days—like joining the Cub Scouts.

I became a Cub Scout and eventually moved on to become a Boy Scout four years later. Dad took me to all the meetings and helped me earn the necessary merit badges to hopefully one day become a coveted Eagle Scout. Most of the merit badges were adapted so I could master them and have the honor of wearing the patches on my uniform. I wore them proudly. The ones that were my favorite to earn were also the most difficult for me to accomplish.

Every summer in June until I was seventeen, Dad and I packed up our gear and headed up to Twin Lake to camp at Gerber Scout camp for a week. About an hour-and-a-half drive from home, I felt like I was in another world—and I loved it.

My week consisted of not showering, fishing every day, sitting around telling stories, and spending every moment with Dad. The camp had tents set up already for the Boy Scouts, but Dad ended up buying us our own tent. We needed one that was bigger to accommodate my chair and one that was better insulated to keep the mosquitos out, since I couldn't easily swat them away. They also had cots for each boy, but I wasn't able to sleep in one because my body was just too rigid and I could fall out easily. Dad got us an inflatable air mattress instead.

One year we had set up our tent on what seemed like higher ground. The whole night it rained, and when we woke in the morning, we were in the middle of a small lake. The water had slowly seeped in through the night while we were asleep, and our air mattresses were surrounded by water. Everything we had in that tent that wasn't on the air mattress was soaked. Dad did what all skilled campers and Boy Scouts do: he threw me in the van and took me home so we could dry off and get a new supply of clothes to take back with us the next day.

As part of earning a special patch for my Boy Scout uniform—and because we thought it would be fun to do—Dad and I chose to participate in Polar Bear camping. The rule was you had to camp out one night in weather that was below freezing, and it had to be near a building in case of an emergency like hypothermia. Two brothers in our troop lived on a farm and allowed a handful of us to Polar Bear camp on their property one night in December. With just our tent, sleeping bags, and five layers of clothing on each of us, we cocooned ourselves up for the night. No heater, no fire, nothing. The temperatures had dropped to negative five degrees that night.

And then it happened—I had to pee.

"Dad, I gotta go," I said, grimacing.

Normally this was not a problem. I got up most every night for some reason or another. Sometimes it was to get a drink of water, sometimes I was stuck in my sheets, sometimes I needed to go to the bathroom. On a good night, it was all of them.

"What? Did you make sure not to drink a lot before we got here, Johnny?"

"Yes, and Mom made sure to give me a pep talk about not getting up in the night for anything unless it was an absolute emergency. But guess what? Nature calls . . ." I trailed off.

Dad tried not to smile, but he couldn't help the grin that was surfacing in the corner of his mouth. He got out of his sleeping bag in the pitch-dark, freezing-cold night to help me. My body, when it is cold, reacts to temperatures differently. Every muscle becomes as stiff as the collar of a newly starched shirt, so that didn't help my dad when he tried to maneuver me. One time after one of my surgeries, a nurse gave us a handheld urinal to use in the middle of the night so Mom or Dad didn't have to get me out of bed. It was life-changing for them, as I was getting heavier to pick up. Now, in the freezing cold, Dad was happy to have it. Peeling away layer after layer after layer, he finally reached the destination . . . and I got stage fright. I couldn't go.

He replaced all of my layers and zipped me up in the sleeping bag. Just as he cocooned himself in, I spoke again.

"Dad, I'm sorry, but I really have to go now."

Turning to look at me, he was so bundled up that all I could see was his eyes—and they didn't look too pleased. He unbundled himself again, muttering something about "bad idea," and headed back over to me. I swear I saw smoke coming from his nostrils but surmised it was just his breath from being so cold.

I still couldn't go.

He thought about waiting there for the urge to come over me again, but it was just so darned cold, so he hopped back in his bag.

Just at that moment, I raised three gloved fingers, and in true Scout-oath form, said, "On my honor, I will do my best to do my duty . . ."

His patience had worn thin, but he couldn't help laughing with me as he got up to help me go to the bathroom for the third attempt, to which I finally did.

Taking me camping in the middle of a snowstorm in negative-degree weather with no heat to speak of surely was a testament to the love he had for me—but getting up in the middle of the night in frigid temperatures when it was pitch-black to help me go to the bathroom three times, now that was unconditional love.

DIFFICULT DECISION

Dad is six foot two, and Mom is five foot two, and since I looked more like Dad, we thought I would have more of his height genes than Mom's. If that was the case, it was imperative for me to keep my body as flexible and as nimble as I possibly could so there was no added stress on my muscles and ligaments as they grew. When I turned seven years old, I went through a huge growth spurt, and my parents noticed that I was constantly fighting the tightness in my muscles whenever I tried to do something. It was becoming frustrating for me, so we made an appointment with my physiatrist to get an idea of what options we might have.

After giving me a thorough evaluation, the doctor rubbed his salt-and-pepper-trimmed beard and said, "There is a procedure that we have had some great success with for kids like Johnny. It's called a selective dorsal rhizotomy, or SDR. It's very effective because it allows some of the spasticity or stiffness to be removed so the child can work on both strengthening and flexibility. It may allow him to do things like sit more easily, use his arms more freely, and in some cases, walk."

My eyes got bigger. The physiatrist saw my expression and knew what I was thinking. Looking at me, he said, "I'm not saying this surgery will ensure you walk, but it may make things easier for you so you don't have to fight against your spasticity all the time. The hard part for you comes after the surgery in the therapy."

My parents had a choice to make. The surgery had great potential to alleviate some of the tightness in my muscles, possibly allowing me to walk. But it also had the potential of causing a permanent loss of bladder control. Mom said she started thinking about the choices she had heard other moms talking about on the playground: *Should I enroll her in dance or theater, or swimming lessons this year or next?* She said she never heard any parents talking about deciding between her child walking or wearing a urine bag.

CHAPTER 4

[Taking Flight]

I've heard it said that some people come into our lives and touch our hearts so deeply that we are never the same again. For me, two of those people were Pa and Uncle John.

Pa lived so close to us that we could walk to his house in just a few minutes if we took the shortcut and beelined through our neighbor's yard. Annie and I got up pretty early in the morning, and the first thing we wanted to do was to head over to Pa's house. Mom would put us in our wagon—Annie sat in front so I could hold onto her and not fall—and we would make our way to Pa's, where cheese puffs and Jell-O chocolate pudding cups always waited for us.

Pa had been married to Grandma Ann until the accident that suddenly left him widowed. They were to celebrate their twenty-fifth anniversary that same year. Mom says my birth was his hope. When he watched me struggle, it inspired him with his own sadness. I made him laugh again and gave him purpose. He did the same for me.

There were many trips to the store, fishing expeditions, MSU basketball games, fixing things together, stories of the past told, and lunches together out on the deck, but they were all to end way too soon. My pa lived only two more years. He died after having a heart attack during bypass surgery. His funeral was on my sixth birthday.

When I was told the news about Pa dying, I looked up at Dad and said innocently, "Maybe now Pa can meet Joe DiMaggio in Heaven and get his autograph?"

Death had always scared me, but being Catholic, my faith taught me that death was a part of life. It was not the end for us, but rather the opportunity to live in Heaven with the saints and angels—and in my childlike eyes, maybe even Joe DiMaggio. I didn't fear death because I wouldn't be on Earth anymore; it was more the ache and hurt I felt of missing those people in my life and not understanding why they had to leave so soon.

The nurse who had cared for my pa told Mom that he had said his only wish was to "see Johnny Boy walk." Several days after his funeral, Mom shared that with me and said she thought Pa would always be with me, helping me to walk and crawl as my guardian angel. She said, "Your body may seem a little lighter for you now because Pa will be helping to push you when you crawl and hold you up when you walk."

After therapy one day I said to Mom, "I think you were right."

"What was I right about, honey?"

"Pa made it much easier for me to walk today."

UNCLE JOHN

I was blessed to have that short amount of time with Pa. When we can have people in our lives who teach without teaching, we are pretty fortunate.

Uncle John was a lot like him. Sometimes, if you are lucky enough, a person comes into your life who is able to understand you for who you are, and not for what the world thinks you should be. That person for me was my Uncle John.

After I was born, it took my parents three days to decide on a name for me. But when they saw me, they knew there was only one choice: John Martin. "John" after my uncle and "Martin" after my pa. They also loved what the names stood for: "John" meant "gift from God," which they truly had felt I was, and "Martin" meant "warlike," which they knew I was going to have to be in my life.

When my parents told Uncle John they named me after him, it was a special moment. And when my uncle came into the NICU after hearing the news, Dad said I grabbed ahold of his finger and never let go.

One of my favorite toys when I was a child was my black Ford F-150 ride-on push truck. I loved that truck because it took me to make-believe adventures where I'd get lost in my imagination.

It had a door on each side, a small backseat—perfect for carrying passengers like Annie's beloved doll named Baby. Behind that was a flatbed. I liked to carry fishing poles there, and sometimes I loaded it with books to take to the park. Annie would sit next to me, and Mom would push both of us in the truck while making truck noises and traffic noises, and on occasion serving as the gas station attendant to fill our fake gas tank up with leaves or grass. During the winter months when I couldn't take it outside, I drove it around the loop that was our kitchen, hallway, living room, and dining room. I pretended to travel to my grandma's house or visit Aunt Kathy and Uncle Rick.

But that truck represented more to me than just what my imagination allowed. It was a truck just like my Uncle John's— and that was more special than anything. He and I did everything together. When I learned to do something new, the first person I wanted to call was Uncle John.

"That's great, Bud!" he would say. "Maybe we should celebrate by going for a truck ride this weekend. How about I come pick you up and we head out?"

"Can we get a chocolate milkshake from McDonald's?" I would ask. He always kept good on his promises. We just drove around town, not having any place to go in particular. We liked to cruise around in search of trucks like our matching black F-150s. Pretty soon, it got to where I started to point out other trucks and name them as well. Sometimes Uncle John would point one out and say, "Look, Bud, there's an F-150," and I would sort of roll my eyes the best I could and say, "No, Uncle John! That is a Ford Ranger." I loved showing him that I knew my trucks. He would play into it as well and say, "Wow! How did you get to be sooo smart?" I used to think that was the greatest thing—having my Uncle John think I was pretty smart. It made me want to learn more.

Uncle John also owned a primrose yellow 1976 Triumph Spitfire. Being over six feet tall, he could barely fit his legs into this car himself, but he still strapped my car seat in the front, and we went for rides to nowhere. It was a sight, really. Uncle John was not married at the time, so I'm sure a kid in a car seat sitting next to him in a little sports car was not really what you would call a chick magnet outing. But he didn't seem to care. To him it was more important to spend time with his buddy.

When we weren't fishing together, Uncle John's hobby was collecting exotic freshwater fish and plants. Because he liked it, I did too. He set up a tank for me in my bedroom with a fluorescent light so I could watch the fish swim around at night. He even let me pick out the fish for it.

I begged him to get me some molly fish. I liked them because they were white with black dots and looked like the dogs from *101 Dalmatians*. But Uncle John kept saying to me, "Buddy, those kinds of fish sometimes want to eat the other fish, so it wouldn't be a good idea to get those." I became silent. Uncle John hated it when I became silent. Seconds later he was pulling out two dalmatian molly fish that I named Perdita and Pongo after the mom and dad dogs from *101 Dalmatians*. Before Uncle John left, we released the fish, and I watched them all night until I fell asleep. They looked so happy in their new home, but the next morning, all of the other fish were either half eaten or eaten completely. The only two left were Perdita and Pongo.

Uncle John also took me to fish auctions, and he proudly introduced me to everyone. It was fun to watch people's paddles go up and down when they were bidding. When Uncle John was ready to bid, he handed me the paddle. I had limited use of my arm, but I was smiling and waving that paddle jerkily so the auctioneer could see me. My body stiffened straight out on Uncle John's lap. This happened several different times, and the audience was getting a kick out of my enthusiasm. It got to the point where the auctioneer yelled out, "Little boy bidding! Little boy bidding!" and no other paddles would try to bid against me.

Uncle John said he would have to take me to more fish auctions after that.

CHECK MARK

It was ironic, really. My mom and dad were determined to treat me like a "typical" child, yet the way they raised me was anything but typical. They did not want to make anything easy on me just because I had cerebral palsy. They also did not want the expectations of my cerebral palsy to follow me through life, but it seemed like it was easier for people outside my family to set parameters on what I could and couldn't do, if they could more easily check it off their list.

One time Mom had a meeting with my special education teacher from preschool to talk about how things were going for me in the classroom. As was usual, Mom said the teacher would pull out my file, look over her notes, and then say something about how well I was doing. She would comment on how I really loved to learn my shapes and how great it was that I was able to encourage others who were struggling to remember them.

Mom said she was always proud to hear stuff like that about me. But then Mom said those good feelings went out the door when the teacher said, "One thing I did notice is that when we were doing a craft with scissors . . . remember those hearts we made for Valentine's Day? It was when we were cutting out those hearts that we noticed Johnny had a hard time staying focused and concentrating on the task."

Mom said she tilted her head to the side in a quizzical way as if to prod the teacher to explain exactly what she meant.

The teacher continued, "Well, that is to be expected since kids with CP have a hard time paying attention to tasks and staying focused. So really it was no surprise to us—we just wanted you to be aware." Mom said you could almost hear the swish of the check mark being placed in the box.

It didn't matter that I paid attention to the rest of the class or that I could sit for hours reading a book. I hated using scissors and so I disengaged. I disengaged because I was bored, not because I had cerebral palsy.

GAME OF MEMORY

I was a good student and had always enjoyed learning. I was especially good at remembering names and dates. When I was about five, I remember my dad and I were outside during a cousin's birthday party playing ping-pong with one of my relatives. Dad was holding me with one arm, and with his other hand, he was gripping mine as I was attempting to hold a paddle. As the ball came toward us, he swung my arm to show me the motion I needed to hit the ball. Just then a man with glasses, wearing a hat, shorts, and flip-flops, came walking up the sidewalk.

"Jeff," he said, "what are you doing over in this neck of the woods?"

It was a former teammate of Dad's who played in a softball league with my Uncle John and him a year ago.

"We are here for a birthday party for my niece," Dad said. "I didn't know you lived around here."

Dad turned me in his arms toward the man. "Johnny, do you remember Mr. Naudi? He played on the softball team last year with Uncle John and me."

Mr. Naudi took off his hat to expose a full head of hair that matched his beard. He combed his hair down a bit, bent down to look me in the eye, smiled, and said, "Hi, Johnny! I remember meeting you at all the games last year."

"Hi!" I replied. "You were number twenty!" I said excitedly.

Seeing my excitement, Mr. Naudi hesitated before saying, "You know, you were very close; I was number twenty-four for my favorite player, Willie Mays, but you had the right idea, maybe just got the numbers switched around a bit."

He and my dad continued their conversation a bit longer before saying good-bye and inviting each other over for a beer.

About twenty minutes later, Mr. Naudi came back with something in his hand. "I went home and dug my jersey out of the bottom drawer and had to come over and show you."

He took the jersey dangling from his right hand and with both hands held it up to show us. There on the back was the number twenty displayed in bold, shiny white numbers. "I wanted to apologize to Johnny," he said. "He was right, I was number twenty! Just for that one year."

My body may have moved slowly—but my memory was pretty sharp.

EVALUATION TIME

My parents had also been adamant on not getting me a powered wheelchair early in my life for fear that I would rely on it too heavily and not use my body to get around. They also were afraid that I would lose a lot of the gains I was making physically, or I would become too complacent in being able to sit and use a joystick to get myself around. They were always wanting to teach me how to overcome challenges because they knew I would probably be challenged my whole life. This way of looking at things sometimes conflicted with other people's opinions, and they would receive a lot of pushback. It even led one therapist to say they were in denial.

When it was evaluation time for me, the therapist went over my progress with my parents and adjusted my rehab plan based on how I was improving and what I was going to be needing to focus on in my upcoming year. Sitting at the kitchen table, they went through all the tasks they worked on with me for the year. It was wonderful to hear the "where I was" checklist compared to the "what I could do now" checklist.

While most of the tasks were small gains, my parents told me that that was okay because they were still improvements and that was a step in the right direction. They had thrown out the milestones chart a long time ago. Not because they didn't think I would reach them, but because they knew when I did, it would be in my own time and not based on a chart of averages.

Next in my evaluation, it was time to talk about goals for the upcoming year, and this particular year—right before I started kindergarten—the therapist felt it was important for me to get a powered wheelchair. Her goal, then, was to start working on transferring so I could learn how to get in and out of my powered wheelchair more easily. "We will also have to work on teaching him how to use a joystick so he can drive his chair in school," my parents remember her saying.

"Oh, we are not going to get him a powerchair right now," my dad said.

The therapist was surprised. "But how will he be able to get around?"

"Well, he will have his manual chair if need be."

She closed the file and sat back in the chair. She shifted her eyes back and forth between Dad and Mom, and then to me. Then she said it.

"You know, you are going to have to get over your denial of Johnny's disability."

Dad said calmly, "I understand this may not be typical. But Becki and I don't want to get him a powerchair right now because we want him to be able to learn first how to get around on his own. We are not in denial. We are well aware of the fact that Johnny has it a little bit tougher than most."

Mom and Dad said it would be impossible to be in denial because the numerous doctor and therapy visits alone were continual reminders of my cerebral palsy. It was just that the approach they decided to take was different—and a lot of people couldn't understand it. My parents knew that choosing this different path might cause more challenges for them, but they knew how important of a choice it was for me. They also wanted to teach me early that it was going to be through hard work and determination that I would have my best shot at independence someday, not by taking the easier and sometimes more common route.

HALF FULL

Optimism was not an unfamiliar thing to us growing up. I can't remember a situation where my parents looked at the glass as half empty. It was always half full—overflowing in fact—and they frequently taught that concept to us. I remember waking up to rain one Saturday morning when I was about seven or eight, and I began to mope because it was a "yucky day" outside. "It's not yucky," Dad said, "it's cozy." And to change our mindset, we made the most of the day by building forts, reading books, and playing games inside.

If something didn't go the way we expected, Mom and Dad always found a positive angle to the situation. Every late fall, we made a visit to the doctor to get the flu shot. Since my immune system was a little more fragile because I had been a preemie, the doctors wanted everyone in our family to get the vaccine. Mom always tried to schedule everyone at the same time since Annie and I were not very gracious about receiving the shot. When we all went together, it made it so much easier on my parents' ears.

This particular time, the doctor's office wasn't able to schedule all of us. It was decided that Mom and Annie would get theirs at the first appointment, and Dad would take me next week with him. So, Mom, Annie, and I got to the doctor's office and sat in the waiting room.

The waiting room was quite full. We took a seat near an elderly man who looked very old and very tired. He smiled softly at us, revealing a few missing teeth. His eyes were kind and gentle. He had on a plaid shirt with a white T-shirt underneath, and his shirt pocket held his glasses. His hands were big and looked as if he had made good use of them throughout his life, because he had calluses on his knuckles. On his feet were a pair of white socks and brown corduroy slipper shoes.

Annie had brought along one of her princess coloring books and markers, and had set up shop on the chair next to the elderly man. I was sitting next to Annie in my stroller. The man kept watching us as Annie colored and Mom started to quiz me on the state capitals. The man smiled when I got the answers right and started to give me clues when I couldn't think of one of the names.

"What's the capital of Delaware?" Mom asked.

"Umm . . . umm . . ."

"It rhymes with rover," the old man said with a wink.

"Dover!" I responded. And we all laughed.

When Annie was done coloring her picture of Princess Jasmine and Aladdin, she ripped it out of the book and went over to Mom. "Can I give this to the grandpa?" she whispered in Mom's ear. Mom told her yes, and she walked over to the man gingerly and held the picture out in front of him without saying anything. His eyes welled up with tears.

"Is this for me?" he asked.

Annie nodded her head. He explained to us how he had grand-kids, too, but they were far away, and he didn't get to see them very often. We also found out that his wife had died several years ago, and to keep himself busy, he liked to do crossword puzzles.

"Do you like crossword puzzles, young man?" He looked at me.

"I like Dilbert," I replied. Mom explained how I didn't do crossword puzzles, but I knew the crosswords were right next to my favorite comic strip, *Dilbert*.

The nurse came out and announced a name. "Ronald?"

The grandpa grabbed ahold of his brown, worn cane and attempted to push himself up. Mom got up to help him stand. He turned to Annie and me and bent down to get as close as he could to our faces. "Thank you so much for talking to me today. You kids made my day special."

We smiled at him. Annie said, "Don't worry, Mom said shots only hurt a little bit." As Mom helped him get to the nurse, I yelled, "Think happy thoughts!" Pa had always told me to do that, so I guess I wanted him to do the same. It was our turn next. The nurse called us in, and then she said, "We had a cancellation. Would you like for us to vaccinate Johnny now as well?"

Panic ensued. Mine was supposed to be next week. I had no time to process! Mom replied, "That would be great! Thank you." The nurse left, and Mom went into crisis control mode. The nurse came in pretty quickly and could tell right away that I should probably receive the shot first since I was starting to cry. When I cried, then Annie began to cry, and that small room echoed badly. Fortunately we were done within a matter of a few minutes, but I was still very upset and mad at Mom. As we walked toward the waiting room, I quickly scanned the area to see if the grandpa was there. I needed to know if I had to "straighten up my act" as Mom would say, but he wasn't there.

Heading back home, Annie and I were still pouting when Mom said, "I know you're not happy with me because you had to get your shot today, but think about it. If we had not gone today, we wouldn't have met that old man in the waiting room. Johnny, you wouldn't have been able to have him help you with the capital of Delaware, and Annie, you wouldn't have been able to give him your picture of Jasmine."

She continued, "You made that man's day. Maybe even his year. He has not seen his grandkids in a long time. Can you imagine how it would be if you couldn't see your grandma and grandpa whenever you wanted? You made him smile, and you made him happy. Wasn't that worth a couple of seconds of a little pinch from a silly ol' shot?"

Mom was always giving us a different perspective, or she made sure to change the outcome from a negative to a positive. If the museum we had planned on going to was closed, we went to breakfast instead. If I was embarrassed because I made a mess when I ate chocolate pudding, we would have a pudding fight. If we said, "I have to" as in "I have to go to school," we were always corrected. "It's 'I *get* to,'" Mom would say. Mom and Dad were always doing that. Turning a bad situation into a good one. It didn't matter where we were or what we were doing; they always tried to see the good, and they taught us the same.

PARALLEL

My parents also loved moments where they could teach valuable lessons. We loved nature and would go out and explore the woods near our house, or sit by the little creek and look for unusual bugs. We loved collecting tadpoles and putting them in a small fish tank.

I was captivated watching their legs start to form. One day I was laying on my bed looking at the tadpoles swimming in the tank. I was about five. The tadpoles were getting bigger now—their back legs were more prominent, and their tails were now really skinny. Mom was in my room getting clothes ready for me for church when I asked her, "Do tadpoles ever have legs that don't work right?"

Conscious of the meaning behind my question, Mom sat down next to me and put her hand on my back. "Yes, I suppose they do," she said.

"Are they able to get around?"

"Yes, but I bet it's difficult for them since they can't use their back legs. They can't hop to get somewhere, so they have to think of other ways to get around."

"Like using their arms," I said. "Their arms have to be pretty strong!"

"Yes," Mom said, "I'll bet their arms are strong just like yours." She reached down and squeezed my bicep. We sat for a minute, just watching the tadpoles.

"You know what else?" she said.

I looked at her, wanting her to tell me more.

"I'll bet those frogs can do anything if they work hard enough at it."

"Like me!"

Mom smiled, knowing I understood what she meant.

We also liked to catch caterpillars and watch them morph into butterflies. For my seventh birthday, Mom and Dad bought me a live butterfly kit with five small caterpillars in it. The kit had a big netted tent that opened up and had a loop on the top so you could hang it.

I loved the whole process of watching the caterpillars eat and get bigger, and it fascinated me how they knew when to start heading up to build their cocoons. Dad used to say it was just like baseball players knowing the perfect timing of when to swing the bat—it was instinctual. I wondered then if I would know when I was ready to walk, if it would be instinctual like that too.

Sometimes I just sat there and peered inside the cocoon to see if I could make out the new wings starting to grow. I thought about how hard they were working so they could have the opportunity to experience a new freedom and a new way of life. I imagined what it would be like to live part of your life crawling around on the ground all day and night, and then suddenly being able to stretch your wings and soar, seeing and doing things you were never able to do before, studying a new perspective but still so acquainted with the ground where you started. I also imagined it would feel a lot like walking would to me, and I wanted so badly to be like the butterfly.

When they started wiggling around in their cocoons, I knew it wasn't because they were nervous; it was because they were excited about the change to come. I would have been too. How could they be still when they were getting ready for such a colossal transformation? They were breaking free from the confines of their body to a new kind of freedom, and it was thrilling for me to watch and imagine what that would feel like. Like a kid who has five dollars to spend in the candy store, the anticipation for me of what was to come was intoxicating.

When the butterflies finally emerged, their wings were all crumpled from being packed into such a small space. They hung onto their old home, as if they wanted to take it all in—every sight and sound was now new to them, yet still so familiar. And they were patient. Patient to let their wings become stronger and fuller. Pumping the fluid of new life, new opportunities, new perspectives, into every vein. They had waited so long and worked so hard and knew their moment to shine would come; they just had to wait a little longer. Slowly their wings started to expand and spread out proudly as if to say, "See, Johnny, it's worth the wait and hard work. Keep at it, you too will spread your wings and fly, just have faith and don't ever give up."

The small, thin, ugly bodies they once lived in became beautiful and colorful . . . and free. Yet, it was the same caterpillar inside. I loved thinking about that.

Soon, the wings fluttered in practice for their maiden flight. I stayed glued to them, watching and waiting. When they would fly for the first time, it would take my breath away. Even though I had anticipated it, their movement still startled me, probably because I was so deep in my own thoughts.

One time as I was watching the butterflies emerge from their cocoons and waiting for their wings to expand, I noticed that one of the butterflies had a right wing that was all bent and crumpled. I waited in the hopes that it would expand like the left one had, but it soon became apparent it was going to remain a crumpled mess. The wing could flutter a bit, but it was smaller and much weaker than its counterpart on the left.

I couldn't help but think that the butterfly was like me. My right arm was much weaker than my left, and because I didn't use it as much, it started to twist in an odd way at my wrist and my fingers curved in and stay crumpled—like the butterfly's wing. In order for me to keep my hand and arm usable, I needed to stretch it and use it as much as possible, so it wouldn't stay all scrunched up and become even smaller and more twisted. It became my mission then to do the same for my butterfly's wing.

The other butterflies were already flitting around inside the tent, but my different butterfly just sat there on its chrysalis. I imagined it was trying to make sense of how it looked so easy for the others to move so effortlessly, but why it was so hard for him. I distinctly remember feeling that way myself.

When I was almost three years old, I was sitting with my grandma on the couch in her family room. Annie was about eight months old at the time and was just learning to crawl. I watched her as she threw one hand out and then do the same with the opposite leg. That movement propelled her forward so she could grab what she wanted in front of her. She moved so wobbly and awkwardly, but to me, it was like watching a beautiful dance. It wasn't like I hadn't seen people move before, but I guess it hit me when it was my sister. I think it was the first time I realized I couldn't do something like others could.

That's why I decided to help my butterfly. I decided I needed to show my butterfly that it was going to be okay. I would help to teach him that having an imperfect wing did not mean you had to have an imperfect life.

To teach it, I put my left hand in the netting and let it climb onto my finger. Surprisingly, it wasn't like the other butterflies had been with me, timid and fearful. It welcomed the opportunity to come and visit with me. Trying to control my movement as best I could, I tried to pull my hand out of the tent smoothly so I could help it better. Mom helped me to steady my arm—she knew exactly what I was trying to do. I knew he couldn't fly, and it would be easier to help it if I had more room for my body to move in its jerky way.

I began to raise and lower my hand so I could show the butterfly what it needed to do to get stronger. I thought maybe if I could get his wing to move up and down, it would be like the strengthening exercises I had to do to make my arms and legs stronger. When I did this, the capable wing excitedly started fluttering, but its right wing barely made any movement. "It's okay," I would tell it, "you aren't ready yet." We usually let the butterflies go free once they had been strong enough to fly, but this time I wanted to keep all of them awhile longer.

"Why is that, Bubba?" Mom asked. "You know it's not fair to keep them in a small tent when they have this beautiful world God made for them."

"I know. I will let them all go; I just want my butterfly to be around them, so he understands how to fly. Maybe if he sees his friends flying, it will make him want to fly too."

Mom understood.

"Ahh, good thinking. Then let's look up what they need to eat so they can have enough energy and strength to show him. And we'll have to make their temporary home a little friendlier for them in the meantime."

"Okay!"

We gathered flowers, twigs, and grass to put inside the tent. We also sliced up some oranges and put them on a small plate in a pool of honey and water. Several times a day, I got my butterfly and set it on the orange slice so it could eat, then we practiced flying again, doing our strengthening exercises. One time when I put my hand in to get him, he flitted a little bit and lifted off the ground. I was ecstatic!

"Did you see that?!" My body stiffened with excitement—so much that my butt was starting to slide off the chair.

"I did, Buddy! He's getting stronger!" She was happy for me and incredulous to what she saw. She had read that a crinkled wing meant a butterfly would not be able to fly—she also knew never to believe everything she read.

After that, I occasionally took my butterfly out from the tent, and he flopped and waggled in the air for longer periods of time. Not going very far, not going very fast, not going very high, and not looking as graceful as his buddies—but he was doing it. He was flying.

That butterfly was me. I was born "imperfect" just like he was with a defective wing. I could have been counted out as never being able to do anything, as not being able to fly. But I wasn't. My parents believed in me, and I never gave up on that butterfly. So, when I saw him flying, albeit awkwardly, it gave me hope that I could do the same if I kept at it and worked hard.

We took the tent outside and released all of the other butterflies first. It was always so great to watch them dart back and forth as they made their way out into the open air. Then it was time to let go of mine.

"You did a great job with him, Johnny. I'm proud of you," Mom said, stroking my head. "You know, letting him go is the right thing. He wouldn't want to be cooped up in that tent being fed all the time when he has this big beautiful world to investigate and figure out. This is what you wanted him to do, and now you've given him the opportunity to do that. Don't take that away from him—let him fly."

Her eyes moistened. Those were words she had rehearsed over and over again in her head because she knew she was going to have to say them to me in a few years.

It was a bittersweet moment as Mom put her hand on my arm to help me lift it, and together we watched as my butterfly clumsily and awkwardly flew away.

CHAPTER 5

[Toolbox]

No matter how positive I am, and how much love surrounds me, my family and I still face challenges. One of Mom's favorite quotes says that life is more about learning how to dance in the rain, rather than waiting for the storm to pass. That's what Mom and Dad were trying to teach me—how to deal with the inevitable storms in my life, and rather than fear them, learn how to deal with those challenges by embracing them, making the best out of the roughest weather, learning to dance with them.

However, what they both didn't realize is that it would be the literal storm that I would soon fear. It all started when I was seven years old. On our way to the grocery store, my mom, my sister, and I got stuck in a torrential downpour. The raindrops were not the kind that made a pitter-patter sound; they were the big, fat kind that plopped down ubiquitously and forced you to pull over. As we sat there and waited for the rain to subside, the storm began ravaging me on the inside. I'm not sure how it snuck up on me, but it did, and it overwhelmed me with terror.

Most people love the sound of a good storm. It soothes them, relaxes them, even comforts them. But for me, storms represented fear, surprise, anxiety, and unpredictability. I started out being afraid just of major storms—the typical thunder-and-lightning variety, a lot of rain, dark ominous clouds, wind. Then my fear grew with each new forecast. I went into terror mode until eventually I didn't want to go outside if there was a *chance* of bad weather. Storms, rain, clouds, they all consumed me, and my fear began to wreak havoc on the rest of the family. In addition to their frustration with trying to figure out how to ease my fears, they lacked sleep and became on edge with each other.

This went on for *three years!* My family soon dreaded the spring and prepared themselves when they saw the forecast for rain. They made sure not to watch or listen to any weather reports when I was around. One time I remember watching TV with my family, and in the right-hand corner of the screen suddenly popped up a little weather radar map that read "severe weather alert" in bold red letters. I was done for the day. Mom and Dad especially hated storms at night because that meant one of them was going to have to stay with me to console me until it passed—which sometimes was the entire night.

They tried so many different ways to ease my fears. They gave me warm baths to help me relax, they had me listen to music with noise-cancelling headphones, and they even talked to the doctor about putting me on medication . . . or putting them on medication! Mom built storms into our homeschool curriculum. I learned about the different types of clouds, how rain forms, what gives thunder its noise. We made our own tornadoes using water and dish soap in a glass bottle. They even had me speak to meteorologists, so they could tell me how wonderful it was to study the weather.

My parents also prayed—a lot. My behavior definitely took a toll on our whole family. No one could understand it, including me. I was a smart kid, and my actions just didn't fit.

I remember driving down to Florida for spring break and having to pull over in Tennessee somewhere because there was a tornado supposedly headed straight toward us. We took cover in a rest area along the highway with other like-minded drivers. I think a lot of those people would have happily taken their chances with the tornado had they known they were going to be stuck with screaming me for that awful hour.

Then one day, it all stopped. Just like that. I woke up to rain falling one morning, and instead of crying, worrying, and obsessing, I asked Mom for breakfast. Breakfast. Just as oddly as the trouble began, it stopped in the same way.

Mom told me I had learned to dance in the rain. I thanked her for being patient enough to teach me how to dance.

AWAKENING

There were other things that were difficult to understand about myself. When I was four years old, I began to display some odd behavior. Whenever I was in my car seat, I took a huge, deep breath, my body tensed up, and I suddenly threw my arms and hands up in the air. My legs at the knees flew out as well, and my facial expression was one of intense fear. I didn't make a sound but looked at my parents as if something was deeply wrong. My body resembled a skydiver falling in the air—minus the goggles, helmet, and altimeter—and my face looked as though I had just discovered my parachute was not going to deploy, showing sheer panic.

In the beginning, I did this on occasion, but then I began to do it more frequently until it got to a point where just getting in the car seat caused it to happen. My parents were greatly concerned that I was in some sort of pain but just couldn't express where it hurt. They thought maybe it was the car seat. They had purchased several different ones to try, but I had the same reaction.

They took me to the doctor for an explanation. One thought I may be having small seizures, but the test came back clear. They checked seizures off the list.

Another doctor suggested I might have reflux because sitting in my car seat was causing too much pressure on my stomach. He prescribed some medication, and my parents followed the doctor's orders, but to no avail. I still would "spasm," as they began to call it, and it was getting worse, not better. We all began to dread getting in the car.

During this time, my parents had been doing some research on a new, promising program that was just starting up about twenty minutes from our house. It was called conductive education, and it originated in Hungary with a doctor named András Petö. Dr. Petö believed children with motor disorders, including cerebral palsy, form new connections in the brain by engaging in motor challenges, peer interaction, and daily tasks in a stimulating environment.

No one in the States had gone through this program yet, but based on what they had read and the research they had done, they liked the idea and set up an evaluation for me.

Dad, Mom, and I arrived at the Conductive Learning Center's temporary location in St. Stephen Catholic School. Inside the classroom were long wooden tables with slatted tops. Small wooden chairs were scattered along the tables, and there were a multitude of toys neatly stored around the room. My parents had prepped me for the appointment, so I had time to process what they were going to do during the meeting, eliminating any fears I might have. They wanted a positive meeting, not one where I was crying.

Two women greeted us at the door and were very kind in welcoming us into the room. "Hi, my name is Ildiko," and pointing to the woman behind her, "and this is Judit. You must be Johnny." They both came over to me in my stroller and shook my hand.

"Can you come over here and place Johnny on the mat, so we can spend some time with him?" Ildiko said as she led us over to a brightly colored floor mat with letters and numbers dotted throughout its squares.

As Ildiko started her evaluation, Judit explained the program to my parents, why the program was effective for children with cerebral palsy, and what kinds of things they worked on with the kids.

Amazingly, I was quite at ease with the whole process. I remember feeling comfortable and safe while Ildiko set me in different positions, stretched my muscles, and talked to me. At the end of the assessment, Dad and Mom were pleased to hear they thought I would benefit from participating in the program.

Before leaving, we were approached by the program director. "Hi! My name is Andrea Benyovszky," she said, holding out her hand to Mom and Dad. She then immediately knelt down to speak to me in my stroller. She reached to hold my hand in hers. That one gesture would be the start of a twenty-year bond we would have together.

As we started for the door, I began to arch my back and voice my concern about having to get back into the car seat. Andrea walked over to me, took my hand, and asked me what was wrong. I was still upset, so Mom started explaining the car seat situation. You could see Andrea was deep in thought when she asked, "And what exactly does he do when he's in the seat?" Mom explained everything.

"Does he do this as soon as he gets in the car?" she asked.

"No, it's usually when we have been driving for a few minutes," Dad said. "We have gone to every specialist we know, and they have all had their opinions; however, what they have prescribed has not worked."

Andrea very confidently replied, "I think he is having a proprioceptive response to the movement of the car."

Mom and Dad looked at her quizzically. "Not sure we understand," Dad said.

"Babies who are born with motor delays or are unable to crawl or walk to propel themselves through time or space have a hard time with processing things that come at them. When he's in the car, his brain is trying to take in all the information coming at him rapidly, and his body can't react. He becomes scared."

At that moment, everything she said made total sense to my parents. It was not panic in my face as much as it was fear.

Andrea suggested they make me feel more secure in my car seat, so my body could feel more stable. "Have him hold onto something to help give him a feeling of control over his movement," she said. She also suggested putting something under my feet for support because it would help me feel more grounded. Mom and Dad thanked her and implemented her suggestions for the ride home. They were hopeful she was right.

Before they got me out of the stroller, Dad positioned his briefcase upright on the floor underneath my seat. They spoke to me about what they were doing so I would be cooperative about getting in my car seat. As soon as I felt something under my feet, my body relaxed. Then Mom and Dad asked me if there was something I would like to hold onto that might make me feel more secure.

"My pants," I suggested. They helped me grab ahold of my pants with both hands. I held on as tightly as possible with the grip I had available. My pinky and ring finger of my right hand couldn't quite open up enough to wrap around the material, but I was used to that by now.

As we started down the road, Dad kept peering back at me in the rearview mirror, and Mom busily chatted with me to distract me. I started to inhale deeply as if I was getting ready to flail my arms, but instead I gripped my pants tighter. That happened several times on the way home, but not once did I look like I was in sheer terror. I had complete control of my arms and legs. Andrea had been right.

Mom and Dad couldn't wait for me to start conductive education.

The program was five days a week, four to five hours a day, and would go in five-week increments. We knew it was going to be hard work, but it helped knowing I would be there with other kids who were similar to me and who were close to my age.

My first day, however, could have gone a little more smoothly. As expected, I had a hard time because it was a change in my routine, and I didn't like that. Originally, they had expected my parents to wait outside, but realized it was too much for me since I was so upset. They invited Mom into the room to stay and assist me.

The day consisted of a lying program where we did several tasks on a table or plinth. Then there was an individualized program where the conductor worked one-on-one with me on my goals. We then had lunch together while working on feeding ourselves, a standing program, and finally a sitting program. All of this was done with kids of similar abilities and similar ages. Mom did not fully grasp the purpose of all the exercises, but she was happy I was moving and stretching for several hours. Then one day, she truly understood.

Every day during the lying program, the conductors had us hold a short dowel rod with both hands. They gently pulled our arms down, so they were stretched out straight near our hips, our hands still grasping the rod. We lifted the rod up and over our heads. Using singing and music along with gentle assistance, we all struggled to get the rod behind our heads. My arms did not want to make that motion, and that rod barely made it over my head and scraped across my scalp on the way over. Mom thought it was just a great stretch until one day she had me on the floor getting me ready for a bath. Mom started to undress me. Then without even thinking about it, I reached down to the hem of my shirt and began to pull it up and over my head. It was the same motion I had done every day over and over again with the rod.

Through repetition and encouragement from my friends, I began to learn to do more things for myself. But more importantly, I began to feel like there was nothing I couldn't accomplish if I worked hard. The conductors believed I could do it—and that made a huge difference. If they wanted me to get from point A to point B in the room, they wouldn't push me in a wheelchair to get me there. They would say, "Okay, Johnny, how are you going to get there?" and I had to figure it out. Conductive education showed me I could be the one in control of my body by taking the steering wheel and letting my cerebral palsy be a welcomed passenger. Since I was almost ten years old, it was a great feeling knowing I could make the decisions that could help determine my future. It was quite a bit different from when I was younger and my parents made all of the big decisions for me. A great example is when they enrolled me in a promising monthlong therapy program in Poland.

HALFWAY AROUND THE WORLD

The program in Poland was called Euromed, and at the heart of it was the Adeli suit. It consisted of a cap, vest, shorts, knee pads, and shoes that were all connected to one another with special loops and bungee-like cords or tendons. There was no other suit like it in the States. It was actually designed for Russian cosmonauts who had been on prolonged space travel. They found when they would come back, their muscles had weakened so badly they needed something to speed up the recovery process. It turned out that the technology and structure of the suit helped kids with muscle disorders like cerebral palsy.

We found out about the program one night when we were watching the local news. I was sitting on the couch, propped up between the cushions, strumming on the kid-sized guitar I had gotten for Christmas. I loved playing that guitar because I felt like my dad. He had taught himself how to play when he was fourteen and used to play in church at Grand Valley when he and Mom were there. Then he started playing in our family room every night so we could have our own little miniconcerts.

As Dad was teaching me how to strum, we heard from the television, "Next up: A family talks about how their daughter with cerebral palsy learned how to walk by receiving a new form of therapy based in a country more than eight thousand miles from Michigan."

That caught my parents' attention.

The reporter asked, "Were you happy with the results? What kind of differences did you see in your daughter?"

"Yes, we were extremely happy! Before we left, our daughter was very limited in what she could do. She couldn't hold her head up very well, her arms stayed bent, her hands stayed clenched in fists all the time, and she couldn't walk."

The news camera panned over to the little five-year-old girl who was starting to walk. Her arms were straight, and her one hand was open, holding onto her mom's hand for assistance. Dad wrote the information down. To help me be as independent as possible, my parents had decided early they wanted to try noninvasive approaches first. They had talked to several families from the States who had gone there, some once, some several times, and they all said their children had made gains—some were even able to walk. After extensive research, we bought airplane tickets to Poland. At just four years old, I had a passport and was about to become a world traveler.

My parents decided it was worth the cost and extreme amount of travel if it meant I had a better shot at being more independent and possibly learning how to walk. I would stay there for the month of June with my mom and my grandma. The therapy was going to be hard, but not as hard as saying good-bye to Dad and Annie.

We met a group of nuns on the plane ride there who had just completed a pilgrimage from Medjugorje, Bosnia and Herzegovina. One of the nuns gave me a blessed rosary, assuring me that everything was going to be okay. We took this as a great sign.

After our eleven-hour flight, we had another four-hour ride to the center in a non-air-conditioned bus in the dead of summer. I had not slept the entire time traveling, and we were wiped out and hungry. Fortunately, the bus stopped at a McDonald's before we arrived. Mom had ordered me chicken nuggets, french fries, and my familiar chocolate shake, thinking that would make me happy, but instead I started crying and sobbing, "Uncle Johhhhnnnnn!" We were all exhausted and homesick already, but Mom kept reminding me why I was here: "to get to do things that maybe you have never done before." It was an exciting thought, but right then all I wanted to do was be with Dad and Uncle John.

My days consisted of a lot of hard work. I woke up at seven thirty in the morning and from that point on was in some different form of therapy. Change was difficult for me, so the first several days were extremely hard. Mom knew I would be better once we settled in a bit and got into a routine. It was my first experience with people who did not speak any English, and that was quite challenging. No one could understand what I was saying.

The translator, Monica, was very sweet and helpful, especially when trying to understand what the doctors were saying about me. I knew they were talking about me when I heard "Janek," the Polish name for John, and I immediately cried. "It is okay, Johnny, the doctors say you are good!" Monica would say with a thick Polish accent, trying to console me.

At night Mom studied Polish from a book she brought with her. She wanted to understand as much as she possibly could when the doctors consulted each other about what "Janek" needed in therapy.

The little town where we stayed was called Mielno and is considered a tourist town in the summer. It winds its way along the Baltic Sea and is dotted with quaint restaurants and shops that beckon you to come in, visit, and spend money. When therapy ended for the day, sometimes we walked a couple of blocks to the Baltic Sea and dipped our toes in the water.

On Sundays, Mom and Grandma pushed me in my stroller to a Catholic church for Mass. Of course, the whole Mass was in

Polish, but that is the beauty of a religion steeped in tradition; the language barrier didn't matter because we knew exactly what was happening. We purchased some prayer cards that had Our Lady of Czestochowa on them. Since she was strong enough to protect Poland, maybe she would make me stronger too.

I put the prayer cards on the wall next to my bed, alongside pictures of other very important people in my life: Dad, Annie, Uncle John. I also had a photo of Sergei Fedorov, Darren McCarty, and Brendan Shanahan. They were Detroit Red Wings hockey players I aspired to be like. "They work really hard every day, just like you, Johnny," Dad would say when we watched them play on TV. "They have to stretch their muscles and practice all the time so they can say they did their best out there. That's why they are the best, because they never give up."

As a four-year-old, it was hard to comprehend why I had to work so hard, but when they told me I would be just like Red Wings center Steve Yzerman or Detroit Lions defensive end Robert Porcher, I understood exactly what I needed to do. I wanted to be like them, and that meant I had to work hard to get there. Before we left for Poland, Mom bought me Yzerman, Shanahan, and Fedorov jerseys. All of my favorite Red Wings players! I wore one every day, and if Mom put a regular shirt on me, I protested. I became known around the center as simply "Shanahan," pronounced, of course, with a Polish accent.

While I was there, I related everything to sports and imagined being an athlete. When the therapists put my specially designed therapy suit on, I was putting on the same gear that hockey or football players wore under their jerseys—it was my shoulder pads, elbow pads, and shin guards. My tennis shoes had to be modified by sewing a piece of material around them with loops for the cords that were attached to the suit. They no longer were tennis shoes; they were my hockey skates.

Sometimes during one of the therapies, I had to hold onto a dowel rod to help me stretch—it became my hockey stick. When I went to the therapy involving weight resistance, where they needed to push and bend my leg with three-pound weights, I wasn't pushing with my leg; I was skating across the ice.

In the therapy called spider, I had to get on my knees and continually sit down and come up tall. When I was there, I was not Johnny Agar; I had to be called Chris Osgood because I was now the Red Wings goalie down on my knees defending the net. When I fell down, I was getting checked against the boards and had to get back up because that's what hockey players did. When I had to reach my arms up high and pull myself up from sitting to standing, I was Yzerman standing up to accept the Stanley Cup. And when people said I was in therapy, I adamantly told them I was working out to get stronger and better to play in the big game. I guess you could say it really was the big game—the game of life.

We had always been a very sports-minded family, and a lot of our conversations eventually led to the big upcoming game or who was involved with the latest trade. So, naturally, I learned to love sports and use it as a motivator to keep working to be the best version of myself.

With inspiration from athletes I had never even met before, I made it through my twenty-eight-day stay in Poland and left there having made some significant gains. I could feel my whole body had become much stronger. I didn't realize it at the time, but making it through that intense program was proof that I could do a lot more if I continued to work hard, stay determined, and keep good role models who could show me how to persevere.

Four months later, in October, I went a second time to Poland with Mom, Dad, and Annie. Dad stayed the first two weeks but had to get back for work. When Dad left, my mom's cousin Sheila joined us for a week, and then Uncle John finished the trip with us. It was a tag team of support and love.

That time I spent in Poland helped me to get stronger, but the help I was getting through the conductive education program now was different. I was ten years old at this point and understood fully that my actions had a direct reflection on the person I would become. I believed the sky was the limit for me. Not many kids with very limited use of their arms and legs would tell you they wanted to be an athlete when they grew up, but that was my goal. In my mind, I had placed no limits on myself.

My parents thought they would need to sit me down one day and explain that I had cerebral palsy. But there was never a need. By having the opportunity to figure out my own limitations, I began to understand my cerebral palsy and wasn't hindered by its medical definition. I defined *my* cerebral palsy. The Conductive Learning Center and Andrea's loving guidance both reinforced this. She had a beautiful gift of speaking in a way that made me feel respected, valued, and empowered. Occupying a body that I felt I had no control over at times was a challenge, but Andrea showed me how to take control of my body by being responsible for myself and my path in life—not by being afraid.

The Conductive Learning Center had many visitors who toured the program throughout the years, and oftentimes I spoke to them about my experience and how it had helped me. This was a great opportunity for me to educate people about cerebral palsy; it was also an opportunity for me to be proud of having cerebral palsy, instead of being ashamed. I could show people how hard I was working to overcome my deficits—and that made me happy. It's exactly why my parents had made the choice when I was born not to mention cerebral palsy around me. They wanted me to understand my body and its limitations first before I listened to people tell me what my limitations were going to be.

The best way I found to deal with my challenges was to hit them head on through hard work, and I began to see that all of the stretching, lifting, and sweat I put into my day was helping me to do more. I was more involved in my sessions and asked Andrea and the other conductors how I could do things at home by myself, so I didn't have to rely on my family so much. One day Dad was carrying me into my bedroom after bringing me downstairs to go to bed. As he got me to the bottom of the stairs, I said,

"You can put me down on the floor right here, Dad; I can crawl into my room the rest of the way."

I knew all the people and experiences I had in my life up to this point had prepared me to succeed. My toolbox was stocked well; now it was time for me to achieve the goals I set for myself.

CHAPTER 6

[Best Friends]

I wanna learn how to play the piano," I said when I was nine. Mom and Dad smiled. They were happy I said that. Not because they had always imagined one of their children becoming a famous pianist and not because they wanted me to follow in their footsteps—neither one of them played—they were grinning because I had placed no limits on my ability. It didn't even cross my mind that my hands had extremely limited movement.

To play the piano, not even to play it well but just to play it, you need to have dexterity in your fingers and hands; they need to be flexible and strong enough to have the endurance to play a song. You need to be able to stretch your fingers out to reach the keys, and you need to be able to move your arms, hands, and fingers in unison and tempo.

Now compare that list to what I had. My left hand—my *good* hand—still had minimal flexibility in it. Although all my fingers on that hand could bend and open fairly well, my movements were slow and awkward in motion, and my pinky and thumb liked to do their own thing, depending on what level of intensity I needed.

My right hand? It liked to stay closefisted a lot—not the best scenario for someone wanting to play the piano. On a good day, it was difficult for me to separate my thumb away from my pointer finger, and when my hand was forced to open, the fingers at the knuckles tended to bend upward instead of downward. Add to all of that the limited use of my stiff-arm movements, and I guess you could say I was not the poster child for piano players.

So, what was Dad's response to my wanting to play the piano?

"Becki, can you call tomorrow to see if the piano teacher has any spots open to teach Johnny?"

No limits. That was our motto, and it was so rewarding for my parents to see I was living it.

My piano teacher, Bethany, was extremely kind and patient teaching me. She tried to place my fingers on the keys to play chords but oftentimes modified them so I could reach the keys. I played most songs using just my left hand, but occasionally she threw in a note or two for me to play with my right hand as well. It was very difficult for me. I had to think about the notes, and I also had to think about how I was going to use so many muscles at once in my fingers, my hand, my arm, my shoulder, and my trunk. They were all getting mixed signals from my brain to do different things at different times. Yet, I loved the feeling of being able to sit in front of a piano and play a song by myself.

Every year, the Conductive Learning Center puts on a rather large fundraising gala and likes to showcase the accomplishments of their kids. This particular year, we had signed on a professional pianist named Rich Ridenour to perform. Mr. Ridenour was a distinguished musician and composer, playing with symphonies all over the world. Knowing I had been taking piano lessons for a couple of years already, the committee asked me to play the piano with Mr. Ridenour on stage. "Sure!" was my response. I loved the Conductive Learning Center and was glad to do what I could for it since the conductors had taught me so much in the six years I had been there.

When I told Bethany, she was extremely excited for me and suggested I play my recital piece, Beethoven's "Ode to Joy." I was able to read notes well, but still had a difficult time playing because of the lack of coordination in my fingers and the limitation of my movements. I had noticed my hands and fingers had become much more limber since playing, but they were still woefully inept in playing dynamically. "Ode to Joy" is meant to be played with your fingers running lightly over the keys—where the notes are smooth and connected. I was not even close. The "Ode to Joy" song I had been rehearsing to play was rudimentary at best. Since Bethany had rearranged the notes to accommodate my jerky style, the song was not the choral symphony masterpiece Beethoven wrote years ago, but I was going to give it my all anyway. I had practiced my heart out—and the moment to play finally came.

ACCOMPANYING

Mom pushed me up onto the stage in my wheelchair to meet Mr. Ridenour for the first time. He then wheeled me up to the piano where he sat on a bench on my left side. As I began to play "Ode to Joy," my fingers knew exactly what to do as I rigidly and slowly plunked away at the notes. But then something wonderful happened. Mr. Ridenour began to accompany me in the song, playing to match my slower tempo. He played with such fluidity and grace that it made me catch my breath. It was one of the most beautiful things I had ever heard.

I found it hard to believe that the tight, awkward fingers of my left hand and the pointer finger from my right were able to make a sound that remarkable. It made me think that no matter what our challenges are in life, we all have beauty inside each of us, we all have a beautiful song waiting to come out. Sometimes all we need is someone to accompany us in life—to "play" along-side us to help draw out that beauty, that song, from within.

My Dad did that for me. He continually guided me through-out life so I could play my *own* song someday. I looked up to him immensely for the man and athlete he was—and I longed to be more like him.

SEEING IS BELIEVING

Dad told me a lot of stories about when he played baseball, but seeing Dad as a professional baseball player was a lot different than just hearing stories. In 2005, when I had just turned eleven, Detroit hosted the All-Star game, and Dad surprised me with tickets. Our seats were in the outfield.

A pitcher named John Smoltz was standing in the outfield catching fly balls during practice. "Smoltzie" played with Dad in both Lakeland and Glens Falls until he got traded to the Atlanta Braves for Doyle Alexander. That proved to be one of the best moves of Smoltz's career. He ended up a Cy Young Award winner, an eight-time All-Star, and champion of the 1995 World Series, and was voted into the Hall of Fame.

Smoltz had a long list of accolades, and while those were all great reasons to be a fan of his, I liked him because of the kind of guy Dad had told me he was. "Smoltzie," Dad would say, "never took his career for granted. He worked hard, practiced routinely, stayed out of trouble, and loved the game of baseball. He was just a good guy."

In the off-season, Dad was going to grad school near Smoltz's hometown of Lansing, Michigan. Being with Atlanta and now in the National League, Smoltz wanted to hone his batting skills while he was home in the winter. He called Dad to see if he would come pitch to him for some batting practice.

In the All-Star game outfield that day, so many people were trying to get Smoltz's attention to have him come over for an autograph, but they were unsuccessful. At one point, Smoltz turned around, saw Dad, and came over to talk to us. It was my first experience seeing Dad as the professional ballplayer he had been, and I thought it was pretty cool. And Dad was right, Smoltzie was a great guy.

THE GAME OF LIFE

Things began to change for me when I turned fourteen. I started to see the world through a different lens. I no longer was a little boy who was easily consoled by his mother's hug or his father's protection; I was turning into a young man who wanted to be as independent as possible. It was a challenging conundrum for me: I wanted the independence, yet I couldn't do anything completely on my own. In frustration, I started becoming very obstinate in my behavior by refusing to do things and standing my ground on senseless points. I sat in my bedroom just thinking or listening to music, lost in my own thoughts about the world around me, my different world, and how I fit into it. Something was missing, but I couldn't quite put my finger on what that something was.

I daydreamed about what it would be like to do things others could do so easily. It was exciting for me to imagine how it would feel to throw a perfect spiral for a touchdown pass, or win the state championship game with the team, or drive a car to pick my girl up for a date—all the things my friends were starting to do now in high school. I was longing for a way to be autonomous and free, and those reveries were my escape. I wanted more. I wanted to do more, accomplish more, be more. I wanted to be like Dad, my best friend. I had heard him tell stories of his younger days, and I ached to do those same things.

Mom said when I was born and diagnosed with cerebral palsy, she worried about how Dad would handle it. She was afraid he wouldn't be able to bond with me if I couldn't throw a ball or catch a pass. Sports had been a huge part of his life ever since he was a baby being hauled off to watch my grandpa pitch in softball games. When Dad got bored at home, he would grab his basketball, hop on his bike, and meet up with some neighborhood kids to shoot hoops on the court two blocks over. Or he would throw balls at a tarp he had rigged inside the garage during the winter, with a wild pitch every now and then creating a dent in the garage door. Dad wasn't just playing sports; he was immersed in them. Sports were not just about a game to him— they meant much more. It had been a way to get his mind off his parents' divorce, a way to stay connected with his dad, a way to bring the family closer together, a way to feel pride, accomplishment, and approval.

So, it was completely logical for Mom to think Dad may not be able to bond with a son whose prognosis would not put him in the starting lineup, or even on the team at all. It wasn't long before she realized how wrong she had been. Dad loved me unconditionally, and it didn't matter to him if I couldn't throw a ball or catch a pass. All that Dad cared about was that I was his son.

Growing up, Dad was a tall, lanky boy who had two loves: sports and magic. If he wasn't practicing one of them, he was certain to be practicing the other. Every year, Dad stayed with my grandpa during "magic week" in Colon, Michigan. The town was considered the "magic capital of the world" because it had been the hometown and burial place of the famous magician Harry Blackstone. Dad watched the magicians try to stump him with their sleight of hand. Ever the realist, Dad studied how they performed their magic to understand how it was done.

In the end, sports won out. He played basketball up through the tenth grade but soon realized he was better at baseball, especially pitching. He also played football for his high school team, the Portage Northern Huskies. When I was ten, my mom decorated my room in everything and anything sports. She had framed the old Yzerman and Peyton Manning jerseys I wore to motivate myself when I was little, and next to those was a brown and white number-eight jersey with the name "AGAR" on the back. It was my dad's high school football jersey. He was a "decent quarterback," Uncle John would tell me. "The problem was he played behind a guy who was all-state."

Even though Dad was the backup, Uncle John said most of the coaches would say that had he played in any other conference back then, he probably would have been a starter. That's why I wanted his jersey up on my wall along with my favorites. Because even as the backup quarterback, Dad always gave it his all.

Dad said he was a good kid who stayed out of trouble and never dabbled in smoking, drinking, or doing drugs—he wanted to stay healthy so he could perform at his best on the field. He worked out a lot and got good grades in school, but he had to work hard at it. His parents had taught him about respect both on and off the field—even when that lesson was greatly tested.

When Dad played for the junior varsity basketball team at age fifteen, the varsity coach required everyone to wear nice clothes on the bus to away games. The two teams shared the bus. His parents were in the process of getting a divorce, and there was not a lot of money to go around. With this in mind, Dad asked his JV coach what exactly the varsity coach meant by dressing up. His coach told him, "Just wear nice clothes."

Grandma was happy Dad could wear the clothes she had gotten him for a family wedding a few weeks back: a nice corduroy tan jacket with a blue and green plaid shirt to wear underneath. She also had purchased some tan corduroy pants that matched the jacket perfectly as well as some brown loafer-type shoes.

On game day, the JV and varsity coaches tallied up the boys as they loaded onto the bus. Once all the boys found a seat, the varsity coach walked down the aisle to scan the players. He stopped where Dad was seated, pointed to him, and very loudly said, "You, off the bus!" His hand made the gesture of an umpire yelling, "You're out!" with his thumb pointing back toward the door of the bus. "I told all of you, you had to dress in a suit."

The coach just kept walking, searching the field of boys. He pointed to another, "You, out!"

And another, "You, out!" Using the same gesture each time. He had kicked four boys off.

As Dad walked off the bus, his JV coach was standing just outside. Dad turned and looked at him and said questioningly, "You said this was fine?"

The JV coach said nothing. Standing there with his hands behind his back, he just bowed his head and began to kick at some gravel under his feet. As if moving that gravel might make him feel better about himself.

Feeling the eyes of their teammates staring at them, the four boys gathered in the parking lot, wondering what just happened. The varsity coach came off the bus with his chest puffed out. "I told you boys to wear suits and you didn't." He glared at each of them. They remained silent—except for one.

Dad, embarrassed but trying to save a small piece of his dignity, leaned into the smug coach and whispered, "We can't afford a suit," looking down at his matching corduroy pants and jacket, "this is the best we could do."

The coach looked at him, scoffed under his breath, and said in a brash voice, "You can't tell me somebody from Portage Northern can't afford dress pants!"

He was right—they couldn't tell him that because they were too humiliated to admit it.

The JV coach kept his head down and hopped on the bus, saying nothing. Doing nothing. Defending no one.

In shock, Dad turned around and walked away. As he did, the bus's doors shut. Dad didn't turn around when he heard the bus drive off without him on it.

Very driven, he worked hard at anything he set his mind to, always challenging himself to do more—whether it was running faster, throwing better, or studying harder—and never complaining or whining about anything. He just did what was necessary to achieve the desired result, adding his efficacious humor along the way. And he always had a competitive nature—competing more against himself and really challenging himself when people doubted him. This was especially true in baseball.

When Dad and Uncle John were little, Grandpa Agar used to take them to a nearby baseball diamond and practice fielding and hitting the ball together. "You have to keep your eye on the ball the whole way in," Grandpa repeatedly said to them. Dad did what Grandpa said, and when he was ten, he was good enough to play with the eleven- and twelve-year-olds in their league—primarily because of his powerful arm.

Dad said he persistently practiced certain baseball drills that helped him pitch faster and harder, and he did these drills until either he was satisfied with his results, or it had gotten too dark outside to see the ball. Sometimes a coach came along and said, "You just don't have the strength you need in your arm." Challenged, Dad went back at it. He knew the only way he was going to do anything, go anywhere, was if he could throw really hard.

Dad's commitment and persistence paid off, but it wasn't until the last two weeks of his senior year of high school, he said, when people started noticing him. He ended up leading the greater Kalamazoo area in strikeouts: ninety strikeouts in sixty innings. He struck out the last six guys he faced to reach the ninety-strikeout milestone and was selected to be on the all-greater Kalamazoo team.

When Dad was visiting colleges, the baseball coach from Central Michigan University told him he wasn't good enough to pitch in a Division I school. So, he elected to go to Division II Grand Valley State, where he would have a better chance to pitch as a freshman and continue to develop. When a Chicago White Sox scout told him after his sophomore year that he just wouldn't be good enough to play professionally, it lit a fire, and he worked like never before leading up to his junior year. He had a good year at Grand Valley, even beating a certain Division I school—Central Michigan University—by a score of 1–0. He even pitched a great game against the perennial powerhouse the University of Michigan, carrying a no-hitter until late in the game before finally losing it.

That summer of 1985, he was 9–1 with the Grand Rapids Sullivans, a national championship–winning semipro team, and was offered a professional contract with the Detroit Tigers organization that year. He stayed focused on his goals, remained persistent, and, above all, believed in himself—all the values he would instill in me. His will to succeed against the naysayers would have a huge impact on my life in years to come.

Some of my fondest memories growing up involve Dad and some kind of sport. Whether it was playing golf with a plastic club and ball in our front yard or learning how to kick my legs and float in our pool, it was always great being with him.

Dad, Uncle John, and Uncle Rick all played in a softball tournament every summer. I looked forward to that tournament because after the games Dad got me out on the field. He held me up at the plate, gripping the bat together, and Uncle Rick pitched to me. We swung as hard as we could. My arms were so stiff that usually my body swung with them, but it didn't matter, I had "hit it outta here!" We dropped the bat, and Dad said, "Run, Johnny, run! Hurry!" He held me up so my feet were barely on the ground, and my legs attempted to run. They were really doing more of a scissoring motion, but to me I was out there running the bases. As I approached first base, Uncle John "hurried" to get the ball, saying things like "Uh-oh, I'm in trouble—it went over my head" or "Ow, I've got a cramp in my leg." He attempted to hobble to get the ball while Uncle Rick waited at second, and then third base for me. Uncle John lobbed the ball to Uncle Rick, who would "not be paying attention" or say that the "the sun was in his eyes" as the ball rolled past him or landed behind him.

As I rounded home, Uncle John waited there for the ball so he could tag me out, but my skills at sliding into home were just too good. Dad laid me on my side as he swooped me under Uncle John's glove, and I was home, "Safe!" Everyone cheered for me. I won the game for the team—and I was never happier than in that moment.

Sometimes, some of my dad's teammates, and even play-ers from other teams, watched me with my dad and uncles and wanted in after the next game. Some guys high-fived me and said, "Great hit," or, "Way to run the bases." I just smiled and said, "Thanks!" It was one of the best memories I have—playing base-ball like Dad. It made me feel "typical."

Yes, Dad was teaching me about the game, but more impor-tantly he was teaching me about the game of life. He was showing me that being a man meant so much more than breaking through the defensive line or pitching a no-hitter. His constant encourage-ment and persuasion, like only a dad could do, was a catalyst for me to do things I was just too afraid to do otherwise.

One of our favorite places to go was to Disney World. That's why it worked so well as a bribe when I took my first steps. It was one of the very few places where we could do things all together as a family. When I was five, however, my fears of the unknown got the best of me, and all the rides or attractions had the potential to make me panic. By panic, I mean I screamed in a controlled state of fear, knowing full well people were staring at me, but it still wouldn't deter me from protesting the ride. I was so afraid of what surprise noise or sight was lurking around the corner.

We were getting ready to go on the new attraction called Test Track, a ride with six-passenger cars that traveled through obsta-cles on a track. My family *knew* I would love it. To ease my fears, Mom took me aside before entering the queue and tried to talk to me about what I was afraid of. That didn't calm me. Then she tried to reason with me, "Johnny, you love cars. You like going fast in the go-karts when you go with Daddy. This ride is similar to that." Reasoning did not work. Then Mom read the ride's description from *The Unofficial Guide to Walt Disney World* she brought with her. "See? Nothing to be afraid of." Nope, still not going. All the convincing in the world was not going to work; my irrational self had shown up to the party and had no intention of leaving.

Finally Dad took over. He walked over to me, got down to eye level, and said, "Buddy, sometimes you've just gotta trust us. We know you will *love* this ride. Now, let's go!"

It was embarrassing for my family—I cried and screamed the whole time in that long line. You started to hear people talking about me: "Poor guy" or "That is so sad" or "Why is he so afraid?" Some tried to help: "This will be our fifth time on the ride, and our little boy . . ."—they patted their son standing next to them on the head and tousled his hair, saying—". . . loves it! I think you will too!" I did a half-smile at them, simultaneously keeping an eye on what was up ahead.

Once inside the car, Dad firmly wrapped his right arm around my shoulders, holding me tight against his body. Our car started out on the track. *There was no turning back now*, I thought. Dad started talking me through the ride. As we went through the bumpy road test, Dad said, "J-j-j-o-o-o-h-h-h-n-n-y-y-y," and I started to smile because his voice sounded funny. Then he said, "This is a cool part, Johnny. Open up your eyes and watch the machine spray our car." When it came time for us to drive along the track outside in speeds of up to sixty-five miles an hour, I was beside myself with laughter, and Dad and I were screaming "Woohoo!" in unison.

When the ride ended, all of the Disney employees were straining their necks to see if I was still crying. I was not. I came around the corner smiling wide and laughing, and they began to smile and give me a thumbs-up.

One of the employees came over to our car, and asked, "How'd you like it?"

To which I replied, "I *loved* it! Thank you for the ride!"

"Do you wanna go again?"

"Absolutely!"

Everyone, including me, was so relieved I loved the ride. The next time around the track, I was smiling with my eyes wide open. I guess you could say Mom and Dad opened my eyes to a lot more than just that test track in front of me that day.

Mom and Dad knew if I didn't get on that ride then, the next one I was afraid of would be even harder. They taught me a valuable lesson that day. They showed me it was all right to be fearful of something, but it was not all right to let those fears take over. "You need to face them head on," Dad would say, "or they will control you, instead of you controlling them." That day, I learned to push myself even when I was deathly afraid. That one "push" instilled in me a confidence that I was going to need throughout my life.

Fast-forward seventeen years, when I was able to walk in the Disney Marathon. The lesson I had learned on this ride helped me conquer any fears I would have with walking. It was a very full-circle moment for me when I crossed the finish line at the Disney Marathon. To celebrate, I asked if we could go ride Test Track.

THE BLUFF

Sports meant everything to me, and I was tired of just looking up to athletes—I wanted to be one. To know what it felt like to shoot a layup, to spike the ball in the end zone, to slide into home, to hear the crowd go wild with emotion because I made a diving catch to end the game victorious. I wanted to work out, not because I would get better at crossing midline, but because working out would help make me a better player. I had been watching athletes for years. I studied them, was inspired by them, knew everything about them. It was not enough for me to watch anymore—I wanted to be one of them.

Being an athlete was the missing piece I searched for in my daydreams.

It had become my other best friend.

It had been with me through every happy and sad time— helping me to have priceless moments that I will keep forever. Pa and I watching a game together is one of the best memories I have, just us and the game. Sports also helped ease the sadness I felt when I had to say good-bye to him for the last time, knowing he was up in Heaven meeting his favorite player.

It was sports that took away the awkwardness people felt about my disability. They didn't think I was mentally incapacitated sitting in a chair anymore when I was able to talk about the big game on TV last night.

And it was sports that came through for me when meeting someone new. All I had to do was start the conversation off with a team they were wearing on their hat or shirt. "Your Red Sox are doing pretty well this year. Big Papi's really carrying them," I'd say. And just like that, I made a friend.

It was sports that helped me feel like I belonged. I became part of Annie's softball team when Dad made me his assistant coach—and now I fit in.

I learned about determination. When I read that a guy like swimmer Michael Phelps, the greatest Olympic athlete of all time, never missed a workout, even on Christmas Day, because he was so determined to be the best, it was easier for me to work hard to reach my goals. Few things come easy in life—sports taught me that.

It was through sports that I was able to understand that failure was just part of the process. I would fail in doing something every day, but it was the act of failure that helped me to succeed. I knew about guys like Michael Jordan. He got cut from his high school basketball team and still went on to be a legendary basketball player because he didn't let all the "missed shots" prevent him from making the good ones.

I would have been totally lost if it hadn't been for sports. It has been a constant in my life since I met it, and without sports, I knew my life would be drastically different—unfulfilled and empty.

When I was little, I loved that Dad "played" the game with me, that I had an idea of what being an athlete felt like. Now as I was becoming a young man, I was also aware that at that moment it had all been just a bluff. Me, fooling myself into imagining that I could be an athlete like all those people I had looked up to for so long. Me, in my spasmodic, mistimed body that moved abruptly could never compare to the finesse of the athletes I watched. Yet, a glimmer of hope would soon be given to me.

PART II

The Road to Doing

CHAPTER 7

[First Taste]

Now that I was sixteen, Dad couldn't pick me up and run the bases anymore, and he couldn't raise me up to our basketball net so I could "dunk one in." Shaving the new whiskers on my face signified more than just a rite of passage into manhood, it was reality punching me in the gut, telling me I was no longer a kid in a make-believe world. I saw things differently and more realistically now. Sports meant everything to me, and when I visualized not being able to participate in them, I detested my cerebral palsy. My disability was never more prominent than when I would think about not being able to be an athlete.

Watching Annie play softball meant more to me than it ever had before. It was as if it were me out there on the field. When she'd bat, it was me batting. When she succeeded, I succeeded, and if she botched a play, so did I. Yet, even with her competing, I still felt a jab in my side like reality kept poking its long, spindly finger at me, reminding me I couldn't play. Even the four- and five-year-old girls on Gracy's team were poking fun at my world when I would see their underdeveloped coordination and lack of knowledge of the game, yet they were still out there participating, while I sat in my chair cheering them on.

What I didn't know is that things were going to start to change for me very soon.

One day in the spring of 2009, Annie got bored and decided to take the dog for a walk. About a half hour later, she came through the door in a sweaty mess, the dog gasping and panting behind her. She had decided to run rather than walk the route, much to the dismay of the dog. As Shelby lapped water furiously, Annie tried to figure out the distance she had run and was surprised when she found out she had gone a little over three miles with minimal effort and no training whatsoever. That knowledge invigorated her to run more.

Almost every day she went out and ran, racking up the miles and lowering her times. Dad started getting concerned with her being out there on the roads by herself, so he would grab his old Schwinn bike and ride along beside her, barely able to keep up. Annie started participating in local 5Ks, placing in the top of her age group, and Dad kept training with her on his bike. Eventually he ditched the bike to run beside her—actually behind her—for a little bit. Then Annie posed a question to him.

"Dad, why don't you sign up to do the Mitchell's Run with me on Saturday?" It was *Tuesday*.

The Mitchell's Run Thru Rockford was a local 5K race that was named after my friend Mitchell Peterson. Mitchell's family found out when he was almost three that he had the progressive muscle disorder called Duchenne muscular dystrophy. They started the race more than twenty years ago to raise funds and awareness for its cure.

"Oh, I don't know. Maybe because I haven't really trained?!" he responded.

"C'mon! You've sorta been running with me. It'll be fun to do together."

The "sorta" part was key, I thought.

But Dad, never wanting to say no to a challenge, agreed. I could see what he was thinking; he *had* been running a bit. Plus, Annie really wanted him to, and Dad would do just about anything for his kids.

Weeks before, Dad had been looking for a jogger to put me in so I could run with him on his one- or two-mile training runs. He thought it would be something we could do together, and he didn't like running by himself since Annie was too fast. We had an old jogger that Mom used to push me in when she ran, but I think she may have donated it to charity—possibly because she was sick of hearing me say, "Burn, baby, burn," every time she ran me up a hill. As it turned out, one of the moms at the Conductive Learning Center gave us one. She said it had "seen better days," but we didn't mind. Dad was happy he could now run with me.

That Saturday in August, Dad, Annie, and I had our race bibs on and were ready to participate in Mitchell's Run, our first race together. It was a beautiful morning in our quaint little downtown. The sun started to show its face over the tall eastern white pines that grew abundantly everywhere, dappling the roads with uneven shadows as the sun peeked through the needles. The city was alive with people—runners wearing their Mitchell's Run shirts warming up and stretching their legs, storeowners cleaning their windows and dusting their shelves, and police officers blocking off side streets for the race and conversing with passersby.

The smell of kettle corn wafted in the air, enticing me to try some Dorothy and Toto's caramel corn. The start line for the race was right across from the Rockford Dam Overlook, and if you got there early enough, you could spot the salmon starting their run upstream—jumping high enough out of the water to show off their shiny, speckled sides. The rush of the Rogue River both invigorated me with its energy and calmed me because of its familiarity.

HUMILIATION

Racers began to line up behind the start. Annie lined up in the front, while Dad and I took our places in the very back of the pack with the walkers. We did this for two reasons: for starters, we didn't want to slow anybody else down by creating a traffic jam with the jogger—and we were going to be slow.

The music playing on the loudspeakers died down as Steve Peterson, Mitchell's dad, welcomed everyone to the eleventh annual race and thanked everyone for supporting Mitchell and others with Duchenne. The national anthem played, and then the starting gun went off. Like cattle going through a corral, Dad and I made our way over the timing strip and were "on the clock." The streets were lined with people cheering for the runners and shaking their cowbells as encouragement. Dad's breath was pretty heavy behind me, and when I tried talking to him, he would wheeze out, "I can't talk to you right now." It took everything he had to get us to the finish line.

As we turned the corner about a half-mile to the finish, an elderly lady came up alongside us while we were running. She was dressed in tight black running shorts that went to her knees and had a purple tank top on with the logo of another race she possibly had participated in. She was carrying a green weight in each of her hands. As she passed us, she smiled and kept on walking. We had just been passed by an eighty-year-old power walker.

Annie was waiting for us at the finish line, all smiles and happy because she had been there for a while now and had time to rest and recuperate. She ran up and gave each of us a big hug and handed Dad a bottle of cold water.

"Well, how'd it feel?" she said as she bounced up and down all full of energy and happiness.

Dad turned to look at her, sweat pouring down his face as he gulped down his bottle of water.

She then turned to look at me quizzically. "Well?" was all she said but implying the same question. I looked up at her with my face solemn.

"We got passed by an old lady who was power walking," I lamented.

People who say you are out there for the fun of running, and not for a fast race time, have never been passed by an elderly lady walking.

By this time, Dad had regained his composure, looked at Annie and said, "If we're going to be doing any more of these races, we have got to start training."

THE BEGINNING

Our friend Chad Spaman was an accomplished runner and tri-athlete, and knew that I loved to go to races and watch Annie run. Chad had just recently been introduced to an organization called myTeam Triumph. The idea for the organization came about when a group of athletes decided there would be much more meaning in their races if they raced for *someone*—in this case, people with disabilities—rather than for their own personal achievement. They loved how racing made them feel and wanted to share that feeling with people who couldn't race on their own.

The people with disabilities are called the "captains" of the team, and the able-bodied athletes are called the "angels." The angels usually participate as a group taking turns pushing the captain to the finish line. Triathlons are particularly challenging. For the swimming portion, the captain gets in an inflatable boat, and the angel pulls the boat with a harness wrapped around his or her waist. The other angels swim alongside. For the bike portion, the captain then gets transferred to a chariot that is pulled by a teammate. On the run, the chariot is detached from the bike and becomes a jogger for the team to push across the finish line. The finisher medal goes to the captain—not the angels.

So, one afternoon while I was at therapy, our phone rang. It was Chad sharing some exciting news. When I got home, Dad told me about the conversation.

"Chad wanted to know if you would be interested in racing with two of his friends and him in the Reeds Lake Triathlon in a couple of weeks," Dad said.

Dad piqued my curiosity when he used the word "racing," and I asked, "How would I do that?"

He explained the concept behind myTeam Triumph. Dad knew I would love to do something like that. He started to ask me if I was interested, but he couldn't get the whole sentence out of his mouth before I said, "Yes! Can I do it, Dad?"

"Sure, if you want to!" Dad said, smiling. "We better clear it with your mom first, though."

We both looked at Mom, who was getting Gracy a snack. "I think it sounds like a great idea if you really wanna do it, Johnny."

I eagerly nodded my head yes and started counting down the days before the race.

The Reeds Lake Triathlon is a sprint triathlon because the distances are short for each discipline. The swim is 750 meters, which is about the length of eight football fields, the bike is twenty kilometers or about twelve miles, and the run is five kilometers or a little over three miles. It was the perfect distance for a first-time triathlon; plus, it was only about fifteen miles from my house.

ACCOMPANYING

When race morning rolled around, I was up before everyone, laying in my bed thinking about what this day was going to feel like for me. I had never done a triathlon, and it gave me a nervous-excited feeling in the pit of my stomach. I was most concerned about the swim. What if the boat tipped over and I ended up in the water? Mom and Dad had taught me how to flip myself over and lay on my back to float—but that was not in a situation like this one. What if they didn't even know I fell out? My tongue started to feel sticky, and my mouth was drying up because I had become so nervous.

We had to be at the race by five thirty in the morning, so Dad came into my room soon after I had woken up. He was full of excitement for me.

"Morning, Johnny. Time to get up; it's race day!" I smiled at him, but my dry upper lip got stuck to my teeth, so my smile ended up looking like I had no lips.

"Good morning!" I managed, as I tried to moisten my mouth.

Dad got me dressed, while Mom woke up Annie and Gracy and started ushering them into the car. Once we arrived, I was amazed at the amount of people already there, setting up and getting things organized in the dark. But I think what I remember the most about that early September morning was the amount of smiles I saw on almost everybody's faces. Maybe it was because of the extreme joy and excitement I was feeling myself—but everyone, it seemed, was happy.

As we looked for the red myTeam Triumph tent, I took in every scene: the glimmer on the water from both the moon and the sun arguing about which should stay in the sky and which should go, the sound booth people checking their mics, "Test one, two. Test one, two." The volunteers were getting prepped on their duties, the medical tent personnel were setting up their tables and equipment, the coffee truck was serving customers their strong brew, and the postrace-area people were opening boxes of bananas, yogurt, and bagels, and slicing up watermelon pieces as nutrition for the athletes.

It was an odd paradox: the quiet calm before the storm of activity flooded the streets and park, but the electricity in the air was enough to light up New York City at night. As we felt our way through the darkened race props of the triathlon in my wheelchair, volunteers pointed us in the direction of the tent, high-fiving us along the way and wishing us a good race.

When we found the tent, there were two other people there in wheelchairs. One was a boy who was older than me. He held tightly onto his hands in front of him and kept his head tilted off to one side. He rarely blinked or changed his facial expression at all. He was there with what looked like his mom as she proudly hitched her arm under his. The other was a boy of about ten who was on the move constantly, so much so I wondered how he was ever going to stay in the boat once the race got started. Just as I was contemplating that, a man came walking up to me, all smiles and cheerful.

"You must be Johnny? I've heard a lot about you from Chad. My name's Terence Reuben," he said in a South African accent.

One of the cofounders of myTeam Triumph, Terence grew up as the son of a pastor who taught him how important it was to love one another, and his mother helped him to understand both the fear and the grace of God. He was raised in Durban, South Africa, during the apartheid years, which made him appreciate the value of every human life, no matter their color, background, or social class. After knowing his background, I found it easier to see why he started such an organization.

Terence had the signature Ironman red dot tattoo on his calf to signify his toughness for completing a race of that caliber. On his arm was a tattoo that expressed much more about who he was as a person. It was an ambigram, an image of a written word that can be viewed in different ways to see different words. When people looked at it on the side of his arm, they could see the word "death," but when Terence looked down at it from his viewpoint, it read "life." He had gotten the idea from one of his favorite Bible verses. Romans 6:23 says, "For the wages of sin is death, but the gift of God is eternal life in Christ Jesus our Lord." He made it into a tattoo, he said, to remind him to always have the right perspective about life.

Terence had an uplifting and cheerful attitude that made you feel happy just being around him, and he always made you feel valued. He shook my hand and introduced me to the rest of the crew, both the volunteers in red shirts, as well as some of the board members who were doubling as angels. He was going to be giving a prerace informational talk in about thirty minutes, but in the meantime he told us to enjoy the fruit, donuts, and coffee.

Soon Chad and our other teammates arrived. When Chad saw me, he smiled and asked if I was ready to race. You could tell he was already in the zone, thinking about the race and its logistics. He introduced me to Phil Vanderlugt and Mike Bieker. Chad would be pulling me during the swim part of the race, Phil would push me in the run, and Mike would pull me on the bike. They all looked like they knew what they were doing, which was a relief to me since I was the newbie.

It was finally time to race. A group of myTeam Triumph volunteers were at the swim area to help me get into the boat. As Mom and Dad put my life vest on, they prepped the seat for me by placing some sticky shelf liner on the bottom of the boat so I didn't slide down as I sat. There was rope on each side of the boat for me to hold onto. My left side cooperated, but my right arm did not want to straighten out, which caused me to lean to the right. The bottom of the life vest pushed against my seat, causing my neck to do a disappearing act. I was so excited to race that my body had become pretty stiff; I could not stay in a sitting position. While the shelf liner may have kept glasses in their place in the cupboard, the piece that was under my butt was failing miserably. Every now and then, Dad had to boost me up. On the back of the boat, in big red letters on a white plastic sign, was the name "Captain Johnny."

Phil and Mike put their swim goggles on while Chad secured the Velcro harness around his waist to pull me. It was that rope that helped pull me toward my future. I just didn't realize the significance yet.

BANG!

The sun was just coming up, casting a hue on the lake that made it look like I was floating in liquid gold. The myTeam Triumph teams were the first to go off in the race. I looked to my left, and there was the boy who had been in constant motion, now holding onto the sides of the boat, completely still. His mouth was agape with wonder, probably amazed that he was in a boat on the water. Just past him was another boat with a person seated in it whom I almost didn't recognize. But upon closer inspection, I realized it was the nonverbal older boy whom I had met earlier. His face looked totally different now. Instead of a blank stare as before, there was something going on inside his mind that had lit a spark in his eyes.

With all the boats now lined up and ready to go, the starting air horn went off. There was a slight jolt on the boat as Chad started to pull me through the water. The nerves I had about being in the boat got left behind at the start line somewhere; I was more concerned about having a good swim time now. Phil swam next to the boat on my left, and Mike was on my right as we all glided through the water as a team. Every now and then, one of them briefly popped their head up, checking to make sure I was all right. As I watched Chad pull me through the water, I was in awe that he would do this for me and felt very fortunate to be out there experiencing it.

For encouragement, I occasionally yelled to the guys to "Keep going!" or "You're doing great!" But every time I did that, my body stiffened up and straighten out, slinking me farther down off of my seat and placing me more in a lying-down position. I could no longer see Chad pulling me, but I could hear his arms gliding swiftly through the water. I could see the bright, blue sky slowly moving above me as we made our way around the buoys. I could hear the crowd cheering. We were the first to arrive!

Chad, somehow barely breathing hard, Phil and Mike high-fived me as the volunteers started taking off my life vest. As the guys went to get their bikes, the myTeam Triumph people quickly transferred me to the chariot. Once they secured me, they pulled me to the bike transition area and attached my chariot to Mike's bike. The volunteers put my helmet on me quickly, and in about five minutes, the four of us were out biking on the road. Mike was incredibly fast, even while pulling my one-hundred-pound body. We stayed behind the police pace car almost the entire twelve miles. I was so happy, not only because I was able to participate in a race like this, but also because we were extremely fast in doing it! I imagined this must be what it felt like to fly.

After what seemed like a quick bike ride, it was time for the run. The volunteers detached my chariot from the bike, added a front wheel to it, and Phil started pushing me through the run while Mike and Chad ran alongside us. Incredibly, they were still able to talk and joke around with me during the run. I told them I had never seen the back of a police car so closely before in my life. They all laughed, and Phil said, "Just so long as you aren't ever in the backseat of one!"

We had such a great time out there. I was almost hoping they weren't as athletically well trained as they were, so the race didn't have to end as soon as it did. We were the first myTeam Triumph team to finish that day—and even one of the first overall. The boy with no expression on his face crossed the finish line with the rest of his team after us. He was smiling from ear to ear. MyTeam Triumph had transformed him too.

Chad, Phil, and Mike all stepped aside so the race official could place the medal around *my* neck. It was an incredible moment for me. Not because we had come in first, not even because I had a medal around my neck—but because I had my first taste of what it meant to participate in a sport. After that race, I had my angels—my teammates—sign my shirt. I hung it in my room next to my jersey signed by Emmitt Smith.

CHAPTER 8

[The Beacon]

After being humiliated by "Grandma," as we lovingly nicknamed her, in the Mitchell's Run, Dad, Annie, and I decided to train a little smarter by joining a group called RunGR. It included beginner and more elite runners. It was great for us because we now had knowledgeable people who could help us with our training, as well as people to run with who would hold us accountable and make it more fun.

Two friends whom we had met through myTeam Triumph, Donna Crowl and Bev Chesebro, encouraged us to participate in the 2011 Fifth Third Riverbank Run, a 25K race held in Grand Rapids every May. The largest 25K road race in the country, it had more than sixteen thousand runners.

"If you can do ten miles in training, adding another five and a half is not much of a difference training-wise," Donna said, encouraging us to sign up. "You could handle the fifteen-and-a-half for the 25K."

When she presented it to us like that, it made complete sense. Adding smaller chunks of miles made it seem possible. So, a few training months later, Dad, Annie, and I ran in the Riverbank Run.

During that time, Donna and Bev asked if I would like to participate with them in the Ludington Lighthouse Triathlon on Lake Michigan in August, just three months away. I wholeheartedly accepted with a smile.

Triathlons are powerful things.

There are very few places you can go where you can feel uplifted, invigorated, and humbled all at once. Surrounded by some of the most optimistic people you will ever meet, you begin to realize that all of those individuals are attempting to do something that has the potential to present them with their biggest failure—yet they are there anyway, ready to accept the challenge. Failure is definitely an option, yes, but they are willing to risk it to prove to themselves that they can overcome what their mind and others tell them they can't.

I wanted to be like them. They were going after something they so badly wanted for a small chance at reaching their goal— even if it meant extreme failure. They did not believe in the stats or the naysayers; they believed in themselves, and that, to them, was worth the effort.

Sometimes they raced for their father who died of cancer, or to be a positive role model for their children, or because they wanted to feel alive for the first time. Whatever the reason, they were there—facing their fears, their demons, their promises—and not backing down from them. They walk around with hope in their heart and determination on their faces at just a "potential," knowing full well that like life, there are no guarantees. There are never any guarantees. The months and years they have trained could unravel in a split second with a popped bike tube, a bad nutrition plan, or a sprained ankle. It all comes down to race day; and even though they are anxious, they are tense, they feel like they are not going to be able to keep their morning meal of banana or peanut butter toast down—they are happy.

I wanted that.

As you walk through the crowd of athletes before the race, you notice the markings on their calves displaying their bib number and their age, and are in awe of the fact that a large lot of them are probably retired, or grandparents, or even great-grandparents. All of them up before the sun even rises. Triathletes form a special family where all are welcome, but only a few want to join them at the dinner table.

During the Ludington Lighthouse triathlon, we fell in love with these infectious people and the atmosphere they created. There was so much positivity in the air; it made it feel as if you could do anything. Dad and Annie could feel it . . . and it got them thinking.

"You know, Annie," Dad said to my sister, "if we started training now, we could probably do this same race next year and push Johnny in it ourselves."

She laughed at his idea, thinking he was joking, since the only bikes they owned were from a garage sale several years ago, and the only swimming they had ever done was in a hotel pool on vacation. Then she looked at him and knew it wasn't a joke.

"Dad, are you serious? How would we do that?"

"I'm not sure, but I bet Donna, Bev, and our run group would help us get started."

Annie was incredulous at the thought, but also very excited at the prospect. She smiled at Dad and said, "I'm game, I think we should give it a try!"

Then they both looked down at me sitting in my chair.

"Johnny," Dad said, "would you want Annie and me to be your angels next year for this same race?"

I was smiling from ear to ear. "That would be awesome!" I screamed. "Let's do it!"

Still uncertain on how to go about training, what kind of equipment they would need, and how they were going to manage all of it, Annie and Dad took on the challenge and signed up to participate in the 2012 race with myTeam Triumph. Maybe it was because of the energy in the air, or because of the positivity surrounding us that day, or maybe a little bit of both, but whatever the reason, we were going to start training for our first triathlon together.

THE ESCAPE

At seventeen, I realized even more that my life was limited. Every day, every hour, sometimes it seemed every minute, I watched my sisters grow to become young adults. I silently observed as they were given more responsibility, more opportunities, and more time away from the house, while I sat there and watched them from my chair go out the front door. I remembered how sad I felt when I was in preschool and watched all the other children dance, play, and sing in a circle. I had to remain outside the circle. It was one of the first times my disability showed its ugly head. I was no longer a child who could become easily distracted by a shiny, new toy his parents gave him when he was sad. I understood the full impact of what was happening, and it was difficult for me to adjust.

I started asserting my independence in the best way I knew how, like wanting to be called "John" instead of "Johnny," but my attempts fell completely short of what I longed for—like an itch you just can't quite reach. Mom and Dad could see the internal conflict and tried to keep me as involved as possible, but the reality was my world was restricted, and I knew it. It was frustrating for a young man whose mind was accomplished, but whose body felt inadequate. I felt like my butterfly from years ago, wrapped up in its cocoon so tightly, wanting to break free, to stretch its beautiful wings and finally fly, but somehow unable to break free from the binding home it had built for itself.

To help me cope, I threw myself into reading about every player from any sport. Baseball was my favorite, of course, but I wasn't prejudiced. I studied football, lacrosse, basketball, cricket, soccer, and even bowling. I memorized the players' stats, how they spent their free time, how they prepared for the game, where they went to high school, how their coaches coached, what their signing bonuses were, and how they mentally prepared before games. I had Mom or Dad pick me up the *Athlon Sports NFL Draft Guide* when they came out on the shelves, so I knew what team wanted who and when. I also went to local games, even if I knew only one person on the team, because I wanted to watch and study the game.

It was my way of escaping the restraints of my chair and mentally bursting out there with the team, imagining what the coach would be telling me, feeling the pats on the shoulder from my teammates, and sweating profusely because I had been running up and down the court so much. Oftentimes, while watching, I would sweat. Mom thought it was because it was hot in the gym, but I knew it was because I had just run the ball down the court and made the shot to put us ahead by two. It was my independence. It was me trying to break free. My days were filled with trips several times a day, every day, to drop Gracy off at the dance studio, and trips to basketball and softball practices and tournaments so Annie could play. It was like I was a pilot sitting in the cockpit looking out the window with my hands on the controls, but never getting to fly the plane.

But this triathlon with Dad and Annie? It was my wings. It helped my imagination soar with all the fun we would have in the training, the studying, the preparation, because I knew I was going to be a part of it. One of the best feelings in the world is to feel wanted and needed, and I wanted and needed that badly.

During those winter months, I was so afraid their plans might change or they'd back out of our "triathlon pact" for some reason. I knew Dad was getting up early to head to our local YMCA to get some swimming in, and I would hear Annie down on the treadmill running some miles, so that helped ease my worry. But every now and then I prodded Dad for reassurance. "It takes a lot of time to do a triathlon," I would say, and Dad would finish my sentence with, ". . . but anything worth doing involves commitment."

I'd do the same to Annie. "It'll be so much fun to do a triathlon with you and Dad this summer!" And she would reassure me with, "Yeah, it will, as long as we can practice our transitions once the weather warms up."

I asked them these types of questions over and over again. I wanted them to know how excited I was, but it also gave me hope they were still planning on following through with their idea. That one single thought was what gave me buoyancy during that long, cold winter in Michigan.

MAY I HAVE THIS DANCE?

My time was still filled by numerous doctor's appointments, therapies, and follow-ups, and my love for sports and focusing on the upcoming triathlon was a great escape from all of that. But the reality was, I longed to be doing what all the other kids were doing at my age. I got my chance as winter neared its end.

A local high school hosted a winter dance called the Sno Shuffle, where the girls asked the guys to go. My family had been friends with the Nawrocki family for several years after meeting them at church, and we became very good friends. They were a close family with four kids: three girls and a boy. The third daughter, Allie, asked me to her high school's Sno Shuffle dance.

Allie was a sweet girl, and I didn't hesitate to respond with an "Absolutely!" However, I was nervous. This was all new territory for me—my first date and my first dance—how was I going to manage taking her out on a date to a dance? Not only that, but dinner before the dance was traditional. This was a big concern for me because while I could feed myself, I wasn't the neatest at it. I had a knack for hitting the side of my mouth with the food from my fork, which left me looking more like the subject for one of Picasso's paintings, rather than the gentleman I was aiming to be. I also couldn't cut up my food myself and could only drink from a handled cup or by using a straw, but even then, the glass had to be close enough for me to reach it.

There were so many unknowns about the dance—how was I going to dance?! I had danced with my sisters and Mom in the kitchen at home before, but Mom had been holding me up, and my sisters held my hands while we all moved to the beat of the music. This dance would be much different. I was not a little boy; I was a seventeen-year-old guy who had a date to dance with. Mom and Dad started going over scenarios with me so I would be ready to respond appropriately. Like, what happens if she gets asked to dance with someone—then what do I do? Or what if a slow song comes on, how will you dance with her? What if someone says something negative to her or me, how will you handle it? I loved my parents for trying to prepare me for the "what ifs," but I also knew this was going to be one of those situations where I had to learn as I went. I was pretty confident we would have a great time. I loved the Nawrocki family, and Allie was a special girl.

The night of the dance soon arrived. Allie had informed me she was going to be wearing a bright pink dress, so when Mom and I went out shopping for a suit, we made sure to get a tie that matched. Dad reminded me to get her a corsage, and I ordered one that went on her wrist since she was wearing a strapless dress. It had white and pink roses in it, and matched perfectly.

On the way to her house, sitting there with my neck con-strained from my matching tie, smelling like I had just walked out of an Abercrombie & Fitch store, with my hair coiffed in gel and donning a freshly shaven face, I remember thinking that this is what it must feel like to be a typical teenager. I had watched my friends go out on dates and had seen them post things on social media about their latest adventures, and at that moment, I felt I was one of them. A minute of normalcy had crept in and made itself a welcome guest in the house of my life with cerebral palsy.

However, as quickly as it had entered the door, it left.

As soon as I went to swat a bug from my face—which was no doubt dizzy from the smell of my aftershave—I was jarred back into reality by the movement of my bumbling arm. I looked down and saw my hands, one fisted and the other with fingers ineptly bent, giving away my secret, and I quickly remembered who I was.

Mom and Dad pulled into the Nawrockis' driveway and got me inside their house to see Allie. She looked beautiful. I had seen her so many times before, at ballgames, church, and family parties, but never wearing a pink dress, with her auburn hair curled so perfectly and her smile so bright. She tried to pin the boutonniere she had gotten me on my coat, and I could see from her shaking hands that she was nervous too. I looked up at her and said, "Don't worry, if you poke me, I probably won't feel it anyway because my nerves caused me to lose feeling in my body about an hour ago!" We all laughed. I had hoped my comment would make her feel more comfortable with me, and it appeared it had because her hands weren't shaking when she tried again.

Our parents took a lot of pictures to mark the night, and we headed off to dinner. Mom and Dad wanted this night to be about Allie and me, not a family get-together, so Mom said good-bye to me at the Nawrockis' house while Dad got me situated at the restaurant and then left. Mr. Nawrocki sat with us at dinner, assisting me when I needed it, but was careful not to do too much. It could have been a disaster waiting to happen, but because of the Nawrocki family and their kindness and sense of humor, we were able to avoid any embarrassing situations that two teenagers on their first date could have had.

The Nawrockis chaperoned at the dance so it seemed natural for them to help me into the school with Allie. Everything I had worried about for the dance that evening went right out the window the moment we entered the room. Allie introduced me to her friends, and I was able to introduce her to some kids I knew. There was no awkwardness at all as we danced and laughed the night away. My disability was nonexistent for a while . . . until I would remember my dad was sitting in the parking lot just in case I needed to use the restroom.

He wanted to make sure that if I needed help, he would be there to provide it. It was a testament to the strength of our relationship—and a foreshadowing of what was to come.

PRACTICE MAKES PERFECT

By now it was spring, and the grass was turning green, the leaves were starting to bud on the trees, and the birds were out singing their tunes, almost as if to remind me that better times were ahead with the warmer weather. Softball season had started for Annie and Gracy, but I was hopeful that I, too, would get to participate in more races with Dad. We had the triathlon to train for after all. Because the weather was warmer, I was now able to join Annie and Dad on their runs and swims. I didn't just have to watch; I was able to ride along with them as they pushed or pulled me.

Since Donna and Bev had done triathlons with several different captains for myTeam Triumph, they helped Dad and Annie tremendously in getting the necessary equipment, telling them how to use it, and training them in how to pull and push me through the course. The first time Dad and Annie got in the water with their wetsuits on, Dad ended up inhaling a large mouthful of water when he went under for the first time. The coldness of the water and the newness of the wetsuit caught him off guard. He popped his head up and started choking for air. "You have to give your body a little more time to adapt to the water before going under," Donna said.

MyTeam Triumph let us borrow one of their boats so Dad could practice pulling something heavy behind him. The first few times, I didn't go in the boat until he was sure he could pull me safely. My first open-water swim with him was in a nearby lake, and I was so nervous. I just kept thinking, "What if he drowns?" Noticing my nerves and in true Dad fashion, he looked at me and said, "Don't worry about me drowning, Johnny . . . the medics can just follow the rope attached to your boat to lead them to the bottom of the lake where I'll be!"

Since their old bikes, complete with fenders and chain guards, wouldn't cut it in a triathlon, Dad and Annie each purchased a lower-end triathlon bike. Donna and Bev kept introducing us to their runner and triathlete friends for added support. One of them was a guy named Jack Carpenter. Jack was an avid cyclist who was also one of the toughest and kindest people we had met. He took us out on training rides for hours, teaching Dad and Annie how and when to shift gears, how to maneuver the bike, how to ride with clipped-in feet, how to repair a tire, and how to keep smiling—even when going uphill.

Annie and Dad really needed to practice their transitions in going from one leg of the race to the other. So, on our driveway they would lay out all their equipment to simulate a race. With a stopwatch in my hand, I timed them as they exited the lake and made their way up the hill past our house to our staged transition area. There they took off their wetsuits and swim caps, and clipped their shoes on the bike pedals. "Five minutes, twenty-three seconds," I would say. "Gotta be faster than that!"

"Five minutes and twenty-three seconds!" Dad would exclaim. "We were faster than that, weren't we?!"

"The stopwatch doesn't lie, Dad. You need to do it again!" I loved being a part of it all. All summer long, we trained until we woke up one morning and it was race day.

GUIDING LIGHT

The weather forecast for Ludington, Michigan, was beautiful that day—a little on the warm side, but no storms or rain. Lake Michigan reflected the beautiful sunrise that was starting to peek up over the horizon, welcoming all the athletes to its shoreline, and what a shoreline it was. Lake Michigan is called Michigan's ocean because you can't see an end to it—it's that vast. However, any proud Michigander will tell you that it's even better than the ocean because it has no salt and no sharks to worry about.

This race day, the lake looked very calm and glassy, which was more than could be said for Dad and Annie's nerves. They were full of tension, not only because they had never done anything like this before, but also because they had the added responsibility of ensuring I was going to be safe and have a good time. They were constantly going over what they needed to do and when they needed to do it, so they could try to eliminate any unforeseen problems that may arise. For extra confidence—and because they wanted him to pull me on the bike—we had asked Jack if he would race as a team with us.

I just couldn't wait to get started. I had looked forward to this moment ever since Annie and Dad said they would race with me more than a year ago. I knew it was going to be a great day because it already was. They had worked hard and done a lot to get this point, and I was excited to be out there with them.

There were three other myTeam Triumph teams at the start of the swim. The captains were Mike, Josh, and Chris. Our friend Terence, one of the organization's founders, was one of the angels for Captain Mike, and he was in his wetsuit, getting used to the feel of the water. I spotted him joking around with one of the captains, trying to make him feel more at ease, and yelled to him, "Hey, Terence! Did you happen to see the back of my shirt?"

"No, I didn't, Johnny, why?" he answered.

"Well, because you're gonna see a lot of it during the race!"

All those who heard the banter started to laugh. "Oh, the trash-talking has already begun! Okay, I see how it is. We're ready for the challenge with you guys! Bring it on!" Terence quipped back.

In one of the best scenes from the movie *Miracle*—one of my all-time favorites—coach Herb Brooks goes into the locker room and riles up his team to play better. After having accomplished that, Brooks passes by his assistant coach and says, "That'll get 'em goin'!" After I trash-talked Terence, I leaned over to Dad and Annie and whispered, "That'll get 'em goin'!" They immediately understood the reference, and we all got a good laugh before the start of the race.

All joking aside though, the beauty of what was happening didn't escape me. We were all family joined by our different abilities, but all sharing a common goal: to feel included. To do something we would never be able to experience were it not for these people, Annie and Dad included, pushing and pulling us through miles of sweat, ache, and yes, even laughter. So, even with all the trash talk, we knew we would all be helping, supporting, and rooting for each other to cross the finish line, because in the end, we were all family cut from the same cloth.

Although Dad was quite winded afterward, the swim went really well, and Annie and Jack came out of the water with us smiling and focused. We all stayed together on the bike as a team, and while Jack had to go at a much slower pace than he was used to—even pulling me—he was happy to do it.

We transitioned well into the run, with Annie taking the helm this time, pushing me through the course. I started singing REO

Speedwagon's "Take It on the Run" as we laughed and joked our way through the streets of Ludington. I was in awe of my sister. At fifteen years old, she could choose a lot of other things to do with her time, yet here she was, gutting it out in a triathlon and pushing her brother with cerebral palsy.

We crossed the finish line, and they placed a medal around my neck first and then gave one to Dad, Annie, and Jack. The medal was a light blue rectangular-shaped medal that said "Ludington Lighthouse Finisher 2012" under a lighthouse with a beacon of light emanating from it. I couldn't help but notice the significance of that. Lighthouses were used to guide ships safely through the night, so they could always find their way through the roughest and stormiest of seas.

Finishing this triathlon with Annie and Dad was the beacon I needed to show me the way forward, helping me to navigate my life with cerebral palsy.

CHAPTER 9

[Framework]

I was always made to feel special, but not different.

Throughout my childhood, my parents' faith guided them into believing everything happened for a reason, that God had our backs, even if we couldn't feel Him near. This was never clearer to me than when I encountered two kids who put that lesson to the test.

I was in kindergarten when it happened. It was on a Monday. I remember because at the beginning of every week, my teacher Mrs. Finn introduced us to a new alphabet letter person, and I was always excited to know what the letter would look like and what its name would be. That week, it was the letter *s*, and the alphabet letter person was Ms. Super Socks. We sang songs about Ms. Super Socks, and all week long we tried to use *s* words in the classroom.

There were two boys in the class who liked to think they were everything. One of the boys was missing a tooth in the front, and the other boy had a lot of freckles on his face. When they were alone, they were different, but when they were together, they were pretty brazen . . . and obnoxious. They teased the girls constantly—especially if a girl was shy. Oftentimes they preyed on me. I guess they thought I was an easy target. I tried not to pay too much attention to them, knowing they wanted to get a rise out of me. Mom would always say, "Kill them with kindness—that way it throws them off and they don't know what to do." That is what I tried to do.

Mrs. Finn did not hear them when they came up to me in class and said, "I have an *s* word for you," as they pointed at me and smirked. They leaned down toward me in my wheelchair and the boy that was missing a front tooth said "stupid," while the other one leaned into me and said "slow." All I remember feeling was shock and then sadness. I had never heard anyone put me down before. It was the first time I was truly aware of my cerebral palsy. When Mom picked me up from school that day, she could tell that I just wasn't myself.

"Anything happen at school today you want to tell me about?" she asked.

"Mom," I said, "am I slow and stupid?"

She pulled the car over into a parking lot and turned the engine off.

"Whatever gave you that idea?"

"Two boys made fun of me today, and they said I was slow and stupid." I was even embarrassed to say anything to Mom—because I felt slow and stupid.

"I'm sorry," she said, the writhing and hurting inside visible on her face. She climbed into the backseat with me. "You know, Johnny, God is using you for something great—you just have to continue to have faith in His plan for you and believe in yourself." She wiped a lone tear from my cheek. "You will always face challenges like those boys trying to make you feel stupid and slow today, but things like that will make you a stronger and a better person, I promise."

Mom knew about facing adversity after losing her whole family one by one throughout her life—and I believed her. It was a lesson I began to understand more with each year that passed.

I began to see I was not like the other kids. I couldn't play like the other kids could; I couldn't use my hands very well. Sometimes when I said something, a line of drool flew from my lip onto my chest or the table in front of me. When I threw a ball, rather than it going forward, it solidly thumped on the ground behind me. Catching a ball was just as bad. When I played cards, my hands couldn't hold them and they always fell in front of me. I struggled with almost everything I did and needed help in almost every situation. But Mom and Dad taught me there was always a way around my challenges and not to give up. They wanted me to believe that I could do anything and constantly thought about how they could adapt scenarios, so I wouldn't feel excluded, but instead feel like a typical little kid.

I may not have been able to play baseball out on the field with the other kids, but I could stand guard at home plate and be the umpire. I may not have been able to be a baseball player, but I could be a part of the team by helping to coach one. I may not have been able to run across the court playing sharks and minnows during gym, but I could get on my scooter board and scoot along on my belly pretending to be a giant crab. And every year, my parents threw a birthday party for me at the bowling alley because everyone could bowl, including me, with a special ramp to roll the ball. I always felt included.

It was not always easy for them to make me feel included, though.

SNAPSHOT

One of the things that is hard to lose when you have cerebral palsy is your startle reflex—that sudden jump you see babies do a lot when something scares them. That's me all the time when I hear a loud noise. Except babies grow out of it. I never will. Don't get me wrong. Everyone jumps when they get scared. The difference between that jump and my jump is about two feet in all directions. My reflex is pretty strong, so when I hear something that surprises me, my whole body gets involved. My legs kick out, my arms go out or up, and my butt lifts off my seat. I have been startled so badly that I have actually accidentally hit people sitting too close to me.

When I was younger, I had a hard time processing what was happening, and so instead of taking it in stride or laughing about it, I cried . . . hysterically. So, you can imagine me at a Fourth of July parade; the sirens, the balloons, the firecrackers, the horns, all of it made me pretty anxious. But every year Mom and Dad packed us all up in the van with all of the Fourth of July parade outing essentials, including noise-canceling head-phones for me.

There was a quaint little town near where we lived, and they loved to celebrate the Fourth. They were well known in the area for their festivals, and Independence Day was their best. They had pie eating contests, games for kids, food booths, a *long* parade, and a huge firework display at the end of the day.

We usually got there early so we could walk around before the parade started. Once it was time for us to go find a spot along the parade route, it was also about the time I started to get extremely anxious. By the start of the parade, as soon as I heard the police car's siren make a quick "bwoop" sound with its flashing lights, I lost it. Mom put the headphones on me as soon as we sat down, but it didn't matter. I still continued to cry and struggle to get out of my stroller or wheelchair.

But, let me tell you, it wasn't easy on Mom and Dad either. They tried to console me, but it was futile. One of them removed me from the situation, but not before they heard the mutterings from people who didn't see the full picture.

"Why don't you just leave him at home?"

"Poor guy! That's torture!"

"Why would you do that to him?"

They didn't see that my being there was a conscious decision my parents made. It wasn't to torture me or because they were being selfish. It was quite the opposite. They were teaching me to adapt to situations, including scary noises, so I could enjoy *everything* life had to offer. They loved me enough to traipse me out there every year knowing that I would have the same reaction, knowing that their patience would be tested with my screaming, and knowing that they would have to put up with the stares and insensitive comments. Those people didn't have a clue as to what my parents were trying to do for me. Those onlookers got a small little snapshot, when they needed the whole album to truly understand. Oftentimes, after the parade, you could hear Mom sniffing quietly in the front seat. It was a hard decision to have me go, but they knew in their hearts it was the right one.

They would ask each other, "And what if we did leave him home?" That would mean my sisters wouldn't get to enjoy the holiday as much, and they loved the parade. Was it fair to leave them home? Was it fair to have one of my parents stay home with me and the other parent just take the girls? *What kind of togetherness would that instill?* they wondered.

Mom laughs when she tells the story of Dad watching a football game when I was a baby and yelling at the TV because of a bad call on the play. I got startled in my bassinette and started crying. Mom looked at Dad and said, "Now that we have Johnny, you are going to have to tone it down when you're watching football, Jeff."

Dad glanced briefly at her, smiled, and said, "No, Johnny will have to get used to it." That pretty much sums up the way they looked at the Fourth of July parade as well—I just had to get used to it.

A year or so later, the most ironic thing happened. The entire Agar family dressed up in colonial garb and rode on the main float for the Fourth of July parade.

I guess you could say I got used to it! It was so much fun I asked to do it again the following year.

FRONT ROW SEAT

My parents also taught me that having a sense of humor can be quite beneficial. Playing catch and having the ball go backward could have been embarrassing, but not when your dad says, "Hey, Johnny, don't try to fake me out with the hidden ball trick! I saw you try to hide the ball behind you just now!" You laugh instead of feeling sorry for yourself or embarrassed. Or when I was concentrating on my writing so much that a line of spit would fall from my lip, and Mom would say, "You know you have an eraser, using your spit is not going to get rid of that word you just tried to write!" Teaching me it was okay to laugh at my differences was a beautiful gift. It had gotten me out of a lot of sticky situations that could have been devastating, like the one time at church.

This particular Sunday was a little more challenging as we all overslept. Mom quickly got me dressed in a silvery blue button-down shirt and a pair of tan dress pants. I have always been a little on the thin side, especially at my waist, and these particular pants really required a belt. Mom knew there was no time to grab one, and besides, I would sit through the Mass, so no one would notice the big-waisted pants anyway.

Once at church, we took the front pew, and I sat on the end of it in my manual wheelchair. It was time for Communion, when everyone goes up to receive the host from the priest. Dad usually pushed me up in my chair to join in the processional line of people, but for whatever reason on this particular day, Dad decided I should get out of my wheelchair and he would carry me up. When he lifted me up out of my chair, I could feel my loose pants starting to slide a little off my waist. I tried to whisper to get Dad's attention, but he was moving so quickly down the pew to get out, that my words couldn't form a sentence fast enough and then it happened—my pants fell down to my ankles.

During Mass.

In front of the whole church.

And I was in the front row.

You could hear a gasp in unison. Mom quickly turned to see what the commotion was and saw me—with no pants on. The first thing she said she thought was, *I am so glad I put on his nice, clean underwear.* As the realization of what was happening hit me, I did the only thing I could do.

I took a bow.

Then I raised my arm as best I could and waved my hand in thanks to everyone for watching. Dad quickly pulled my pants up and held them tightly through the rest of the line.

SHHH!

I found that this sense of humor was especially useful as I continued to get older. In the fall of 2014, I enrolled at Aquinas College, a small Catholic liberal arts college that was close to home. It's not surprising that I had a dual major in sports management and business administration. Mom would drop me off at my class, wait for it to finish, then take me to my next one—and repeat the process until I graduated five years later. She did that because it was somewhat of a dangerous situation for me to drive my chair by myself around campus. I can't see depth, so curbs, trees, and people's feet are in danger when I drive. I also have very minimal peripheral vision—which was just a bonus. This particular day, I was on my way to a sport management meeting at the campus library—and I was driving.

The library had metal detectors to navigate at the entrance. Mom was talking to someone in the hallway outside the entrance, and some of the board members of Aquinas were coming out of a conference room after a meeting. As the president of the college waved to me, I ran smack dab into the detector, bringing my powerchair to a bouncing halt and making an extremely loud noise in the process. All eyes on me, I simply looked up and said, "Just wanted to make sure those were securely in the ground, so no one hurt themselves. It looks like everyone is safe here."

BIG RED

Sometimes before class at Aquinas, I chewed a piece of gum to help me concentrate. My favorite was Big Red cinnamon gum. Halfway through my humanities class, ironically, my jaw became tired of chewing, so I spit it out into a trash can that was sitting next to my wheelchair. Unfortunately, I missed the can and the gum landed in a pink blob on my lap. Trying not to make a scene and being very quiet, I picked the gum up with my left pointer finger and thumb. As is the case with most people with cerebral palsy, we don't have a lot of control with the strength in our fingers, so rather than pick the gum up gingerly, I crushed it with my pincer grasp. The death grip I had on it only made the matter worse as the gum became a stringy mess between my fingers.

I struggled with the limited use I have in my right arm to take the gum from my left hand, but it proved to be a desperate attempt as I now had some of the gum between both fingers on both hands. Like a spider had spun a web, the gum left a trail of pink webbing across my body. I quickly put my left hand down in order to get the majority of gum off onto my pants before anyone could see, but it just created more of a web on the front of my body and across my lap. By this time, class had ended, and my mom walked in to get me. She stopped dead in her tracks and gasped at the sight of me. I had an intricate series of interconnected red string running from my mouth to my knees, as well as on my wheelchair controls and seat.

"What happened to you?!" Mom snorted as she tried futilely to get me out of anyone's line of sight. Then I responded, "Don't worry, Mom, a girl in class already took a picture of me. I'm sure it will be posted on Instagram within the next couple of minutes."

We began to laugh at the hilarity of the situation. To the select few who were in the room that day and witnessed my gum fiasco, I became forever known as "Big Red."

ALL SMILES

The idea of walking the last mile of a race came to me one night when I was lying in bed thinking about a million different things, as my mind loved to do. My thoughts had been tuned into the Tigers game I was going to watch on TV the next day. I thought about the game of baseball and why I loved it so much. Was it because every time a player went up to bat, there was a significant chance he would strike out? Even the greatest players—those who are in the Hall of Fame—succeed only three out of every ten times at bat, which means they fail 70 percent of the time. Yet they continue to get up there and face the pitcher again and again, knowing this next time could be the game-winning hit. Not only that, but each time they go up to the plate, they swing hard; they aren't afraid of failing or of being embarrassed by a miss. They give it their all just in case they get a hit. Just like in life, they are willing to take a swing at whatever chance they get even though the odds say they will probably fail.

Or, I thought, *Do I like baseball because it has 162 games in the season, which means their season is like a marathon rather than a sprint?* In that way, teams can struggle in the beginning but can turn things around by the end of the season. That says to me that it doesn't matter how you start; what matters is where you end up, and through hard work and determination, you have the opportunity to change things around. Then I thought about the challenges I had in my life as an eighteen-year-old and how I had to be diligent with constantly improving myself—or I would never get better. Like one of my favorite players Justin Verlander does. He has mental toughness unlike most. As the game goes on, his pitching becomes stronger. That's how I needed to be.

And that's when I decided I was going to walk a mile in a race.

I had a sudden urge to stop dreaming about what it would feel like to be an athlete, and to try to be one. To take a swing at it. If I missed, what would happen? I would fail? I was used to that already—I failed over and over again on a daily basis. But if I succeeded, I would get to know what it felt like to cross a finish line on my own two feet.

The next morning was a rainy and cloudy day, but it didn't matter because I was too happy to even care. I had a new lease on life, and I couldn't wait to share my idea with Mom and Dad.

Sitting at the breakfast table, I was all smiles like a little boy on Christmas morning. While Mom was pouring me some milk, Dad was just taking a seat at the table. Mom had always pushed for us to eat meals together as a family. She had talked to a Jesuit priest years ago who had told her the one thing he noticed about families who were able to remain close is, besides praying, they all ate meals together. Mom said it was the one time we could catch up on each other's lives and what was on our minds. This morning, I definitely had something I wanted to catch them up on.

Annie and Gracy took their usual seats at the table, still in their pajamas and half asleep. We said grace and started passing food around. Mom immediately noticed that something was up. My jerky, stiff movements and the smile on my face gave me away.

"Why is Johnny so happy?" Annie asked.

"I don't know," Dad responded.

"Someone must have had a good dream last night!" Mom said.

Maybe that was it. Had I dreamed everything last night? Was I really going to do this? It felt like a dream, but I knew it was real. It was very real.

I couldn't contain my excitement any longer. "Last night, I was thinking."

"Wow! Mark this date on the calendar; Johnny was actually thinking!" Gracy said, cutting me no slack.

"I had an idea. I want to walk a mile in the St. Pat's 5K."

They all looked at me stunned. I continued, "I was thinking last night that I wanted to know what it felt like to be an athlete. I know all about them, but to actually work toward something like they do, well, they aren't afraid of the hard work or the potential to fail.

"Plus, I thought it would be nice to give Dad a break for a little while."

Mom's eyes filled with tears, and Annie and Gracy became silent and motionless. Dad looked at me and had to clear his throat before speaking.

"Wow," he said. "That's a pretty big task to take on. You'll have to start training right away; the race is about a year out."

I loved my family. Not one of them tried to dissuade me from such a big dream that seemed nearly impossible to fulfill. The most I had ever walked in my walker was twenty-three steps.

Twenty-three steps.

How in the world was I going to walk a mile after only walking twenty-three steps? If I thought about it too long, I would have convinced myself it was a pipe dream. I was so sure about the idea in the middle of the night, but now it was daylight, and the reality of my world was staring at me in the face. Had they said one thing, just one thing to try to dissuade me from such an imaginative idea, I might have backed out. I might have questioned what I was thinking too much and filed my dream back into the drawer where all unfulfilled dreams go, never to be opened again. But they didn't. Rather, they encouraged me by telling me I had "better start training."

Dad told me later he tried to calculate how many steps it would take for me to complete a mile and lost count.

CHAPTER 10

[Walk of Faith]

Our church could be on a postcard. I'm serious! St. Patrick Parish is in a traditional white church building, with stained glass windows lining every side, and a tall, pointed steeple. A country cemetery sits just outside the front door, and the church itself is surrounded by green fields and apple and dairy farms.

Each summer—for almost one hundred years now—St. Patrick holds a parish festival to raise money for its school and to celebrate our faith and our community. Since our church is located within a farming community, parishioners drive their antique tractors and display them on the grass, along with antique or rare cars. With poker and blackjack at Vegas Night, a beer tent, game booths for the kids, and live music, there's always plenty to do. And I haven't even mentioned the silent and live auctions where people bid on things like homemade pies for a year.

At the start of this three-day festival is always a 5K run/walk, now organized by our friend Jen Post. It's funny: for a church putting on a casual run/walk in middle-of-nowhere Michigan, we still have two illustrious runners. Greg Meyer is known among the parishioners as a guy with a great sense of humor who always shows up to 8:00 a.m. Mass, but to the world outside, he is the last American-born runner to win the Boston Marathon. And his good friend Dathan Ritzenhein was a three-time national cross-country champion and Olympic long-distance runner. I always made sure to position my wheelchair at the end of the course so I could watch them finish.

Of course, I'd told Mrs. Post that I was planning on walking in the St. Patrick 5K. One Sunday after Mass she approached me.

"Johnny, I was wondering if you would do me a favor?"

"Sure!" I smiled. "Anything for you!" Sometimes I say that without knowing what I'm agreeing to, which can be dangerous.

She smiled back. "Well, I was hoping to get more people involved in the race this year. I thought it would be a good idea to see if after every Mass, you would be up for encouraging people to participate, since you're going to be walking in it."

"I would *love* to do that for you!" Phew. Talking about sports in front of people was right up my alley.

I spoke at a total of three Masses, and at each I had a killer sales pitch. "Listen, if *I* can be out there walking in it, I think all of *you* can participate as well, and help support our church and school!"

Coming from me, that good ol' Catholic guilt hit the spot, and Mrs. Post let me know the sign-ups were higher than ever.

But with that job off my mind, I knew I needed to focus on the *real* task at hand: training. There wasn't much time left to prepare for what we were calling my "marathon mile."

TWENTY-THREE STEPS

When I was three years old, I had proven to myself that if I was determined enough to go after a goal, I could reach it with the right motivation. That's when I had walked those initial two steps to go to Disney World. Once I had decided to walk that mile, my motivation surpassed logic. I wanted to feel like an athlete. So, I began to train, or should I say, I began to *learn* how to train.

In my head, I knew exactly what I needed to do to prepare to walk this mile. I had watched and studied athletes for years. I knew you had to work hard (check) and be determined (check), goal focused (check), motivated (check), resilient (check), and good under pressure (check). I had this, no problem. What I didn't have was a clue!

It is one thing to study how to be an athlete, but it's a totally different concept to apply all those methods in your training. My first instinct was to go big. I wanted to start walking the minute I made my decision. When Mom wanted to write out a training schedule, my answer was, "Every day!" When she wanted to stretch me first, I was impatient and just wanted to get moving. One of the first times out on a training walk with Dad, I began to grimace a bit. Dad noticed immediately.

"What's wrong, Johnny?"

"Nothing," I lied.

"Johnny, you're walking slower and dragging your left foot. Is your hip hurting?" Dad questioned.

"It's okay," I said. "I can push through the pain."

Dad immediately stopped me, and we headed back home. I was extremely mad. Mad because I had seen him executing his exercises in training, and I wanted to do the same. I wanted to grind through the pain like I had seen so many athletes do when pushed to the limit. I was furious because I thought he was treating me "special" and wouldn't allow me to tough it out. I didn't realize he was actually helping me.

As I sulked, Dad explained, "Your mom and I have raised you your whole life to not use your CP as an excuse for anything; this is no different. But, you have to listen to your body just like every athlete does. When they feel they are pushing too much, they have to stop, or they will injure themselves too."

I had never thought of that. I had gone down my checklist in my head—and that wasn't on it.

Listening to my body was a foreign concept to me. I needed to understand that it was going to take me longer to accomplish my goals. I needed to go back to the principle that it's not a bad thing to move at my body's pace; it was just going to take me longer to get there . . . but I could still get there. I smiled then, because I realized I had just had my first lesson *as an athlete*.

We had a schedule for my training. Three days a week, I stretched and did core exercises, including sit-ups and Supermans. We also did an exercise we learned in Poland called coola-loo-loos. I laid on my back and my mom brought my knees to my chest. From there, I wrapped my arms around my legs while lifting my head, and she rocked me back and forth and around. Sort of like a cannonball, but with no water. Sometimes on those days I lifted weights to strengthen my legs and shoulders. It was important for my upper body to have strength because it had to support a lot of my weight when walking in my walker.

I liked to base my training off what Dad was doing with our RunGR group. That meant walking Tuesdays, Thursdays, and Saturdays. Since winters are brutal in Michigan, I could only walk when there was no snow on the ground or when the temperature was in the forties—and even then I had to layer so many clothes I could barely move. The cold also tightens up my muscles, so we could only walk briefly. The majority of winter walks would be inside our local YMCA on the track.

I wear AFOs, which are braces that fit underneath the length of my foot and go up to my knee. Over those I wear high-top shoes that help support my ankle and give me even more stability. Long tube socks or compression socks help considerably to avoid the rubbing and sweating that occurs because of the braces. I have to keep my fingernails trimmed to avoid cutting the skin in my palm because my grip is so tight.

By far, one of the most important elements of my training is my preworkout music. I listen to five different songs over and over again: "Dreams" by Van Halen, "Feels Like Today" by Rascal Flatts, "Run On" by Elvis Presley, "Don't Stop Believing" by Journey, and Kid Rock's "Born Free." Kid Rock's lyrics especially hit me hard: "You can knock me down and watch me bleed, but you can't keep no chains on me. I was born free." My cerebral palsy wanted to chain me down, but my mind was born free.

The messages in these songs had a tremendous effect on my ability to get up every day, face the challenges ahead, and stay motivated and focused to achieve my goals. There were many times when I didn't want to train, but I thought of Phelps, who never stopped a day to train because he was so dedicated to reaching his goals. I soon learned, if I took a day off, it took me longer to make progress because my body wouldn't respond as well, which meant it took longer for me to reach my goal. Training to walk this mile was important to me for one big reason: it taught me about myself and my capabilities, and gave me a greater sense of accomplishment to aid me in progressing forward in life.

Walking for me is extremely difficult, physically and mentally. I have to think about every movement and concentrate on the sequence of actions. Bend my left knee and step out with my right foot, plant, and shift my weight onto my right foot. Keep my hands on the walker for balance, bend my right knee, and repeat, over and over . . . all the while keeping my trunk centered, holding my head up, looking straight ahead, pushing the walker forward, and breathing deeply.

It was exhausting just *writing* that paragraph, so imagine how it feels to put it into action!

I used to watch my sister Gracy when she was learning how to walk. I was dumbfounded by the ease with which she learned. Sure, she fell a lot, but the coordination she had to be able to get back up again astonished me. It took her a month to accomplish a task I'd been working on for almost all of my life.

Previous to my year of training, the farthest I'd ever walked at once was twenty-three steps—which is why the idea of walking a *mile* seemed so crazy to everyone. Including me!

I remember the time I walked those twenty-three steps like it happened yesterday. They say your senses are keen when experiencing something shocking, and my senses were on high alert. It was nearing the end of the day at the Conductive Learning Center, and the late afternoon sun was just starting to peek through the front door. I could smell spaghetti in the air. The early childhood class had left, so it was just our group of adolescents. Nathaniel was working on being able to get upstairs, Matt was working on bending his knees more, and Sarah was working on her balance. My goal was to keep my form while walking to the end of the hallway.

Since it was the end of the day, my muscles were already limber from the five hours of work I had put in already. Andrea was behind me on a rolling footstool to help me in bending my knees or to position my foot when I stepped. My inner thigh muscles were so tight that they liked to pull my legs inward, which made them cross over each other. To alleviate this, the conductors had designed a length of PVC pipe that attached to the frame of my walker. That way, when I stepped, I had the pipe there to help me avoid tangling my feet. "One, *two*, one, *two*," Andrea chanted to cue my feet and to keep me in rhythm. "That's it, *János!* Good job! *Nagyon jó!*"

Her Hungarian had rubbed off to the point where I understood the language and could speak it a little. "*Kösonöm szépen,*" I grunted back at her. That meant "thank you very much."

However, by the time I reached the halfway point of the hallway, I thought my body was done. I was sweating, my arms were tired from having to use them to support my weight so much, and my legs were feeling pretty heavy.

Just then, someone shouted some encouraging words, which helped me walk a few more steps—and then another shout helped me walk *another* few steps. We always encouraged each other, and their words gave me just the push I needed to finish the task I had started. And two steps later, I noticed I had made it to the end of the hallway! Extremely winded, heart pounding, and sweaty, but I made it.

"*Ügyes vagy, János!*" Andrea crowed, and provided a chair for me to sit and rest. She was telling me "nice work!"

When Mom came to pick me up several minutes later, I shouted the good news, "I just walked twenty-three steps in my walker!"

Mom's mouth fell open in amazement, and she wrapped her arms around me. "How did it feel?"

"Really good," I said. "But *really* tiring."

"Ready for a nap . . . and then back to working on it tomorrow?" she asked with encouragement in her voice.

"Right now," I joked, "I think I am going to need to get in the tub because I don't think I smell too good after sweating so much!"

On our way home, Mom reminded me what I had just done. "Not only did you do something that *no one* used to think you could ever do," she said, "but you did it twenty-three times!"

All the hard work was paying off. The time I was putting in at the center, the encouragement from my peers, the belief from my parents, all had contributed significantly in helping me to do things that were beyond anything I was able to do before. I was also becoming stronger. My parents ultimately made the difficult decision to go ahead with the SDR surgery. They reasoned that the benefits far outweighed the risks. It helped increase my strength and flexibility, and allowed me to learn how to work with my muscles, rather than fight the tightness constantly.

As she called Dad to tell him the good news, I mulled over my recent accomplishment. I had proven to myself that I had a lot more in me than even *I* knew. I had wanted so badly to quit halfway through, but I'd stayed focused on my goal. I made mental notes about what worked for me: knowing my goal, being encouraged, and not focusing on the negatives my body was screaming but rather on how good I would feel once I reached my goal.

And, most importantly, believing in myself—that was key.

When Mom put the phone on speaker, I could tell how excited Dad was. "I'm blown away, but I always knew you could do it, Johnny!" he said.

"ARE YOU READY, JOHNNY BOY?"

June in Michigan is always beautiful, and that year we had one of the best slices of Michigan pie ever, right in time for the St. Patrick 5K. Legend has it that, back in the day, traveling priests brought back different species of trees as they crisscrossed the country on horseback and planted them on the grounds of St. Patrick. Whether that was true or not, walking through the Stations of the Cross—a series of fourteen prayer areas to commemorate Jesus's last days—you would see maple, cedar, black cherry, hemlock, oak, aspen, and even some sixty-foot-tall hickory trees that drop nuts onto Father Mark's front lawn right next door to the church.

The windows of Father Mark's rectory looked out on the parish cemetery. Speckled with Irish names—many of whom founded our church hundreds of years ago—and Celtic crosses, the headstones serve as a reminder that life is a gift and to use every day wisely. Sometimes when the evening sun lit up the gravestones at the end of the day, I felt like God was telling me not to worry—that even through death, He would be victorious.

I hoped I would be victorious in a much smaller way! It was race day. The route was a simple out-and-back, beginning and ending on the street in front of the church. Official start time was 7:00 p.m., but just like Mass on Sunday, people loved to gather early and stay late, chatting and catching up. Besides, it was the height of summer, and it would stay light until almost ten at night.

Dad, Mom, Annie, Gracy, and I arrived early as well. We needed to place my walker at the one-mile-remaining mark, facing the church, so it would be waiting for me when I needed it. Our plan was to have Dad and me start the race together. He would push me for the first two miles, and then he would get me out of my jogger and put me in my walker, and I'd walk the remaining mile to the finish line.

Father Mark was greeting people as they arrived at the starting line. When he saw me, he made a beeline for my jogger. "It's gonna be a good race," he enthused. "Are you ready, Johnny Boy?!"

"Sure am, Father!" Everybody loved Father Mark. He was a real people person. I smiled at him. "I see you were praying extra hard for nice weather for race day!"

"I tried my best, Johnny, that's for sure."

"I'm going to try and do the same out there today, Father. Hopefully by the end of the race, I won't be across the street with our founders, though!" I quipped, nodding my head at the cemetery.

Father Mark started laughing. "I have been praying for you a lot, Johnny Boy. You are going to be okay out there today. You got this! I will look for you out on the course!"

I was so thankful for his friendship and guidance—and relieved to have someone else looking out for me during the race.

Soon thereafter, some of my extended family arrived. My aunts and uncles and cousins all cheered me on with smiles, shouts, and hand-drawn signs. Numerous friends from our RunGR group, including my coach Woj, showed up as well. My heart swelled up with gratitude for all the support and encouragement. It's hard to do something difficult alone, but when you're surrounded by the love of family and friends, it makes the journey so much sweeter.

We lined up with all the other runners. One of the middle schoolers sang the national anthem, and Father gave the blessing over the race and its participants. I could feel my heart pumping hard—was it the same prerace or pregame feeling athletes experienced? It had started to rain slightly, which was a welcome relief from the summer heat.

Okay, Johnny, I told myself. *Father Mark is right. You've got this. You're ready.*

IMPOSSIBLE MILE

Bang!

We were on our way. I felt pats on my shoulder and heard things like, "Good luck today, Johnny!" or "We'll be waitin' for you at the finish, Johnny!"

I must have asked Dad five or six times if he was sure my walker was where it needed to be, and every time he reassured me it was. I went over in my head what I needed to do: shift my weight, keep my head up, bend at the knee, breathe. I reminded myself that Mom and Dad had taught me that it was through facing challenges that I would become stronger.

As I looked at the church steeple, rising over the trees but shrinking in the distance, I thought about my faith. It had gotten me through so much already. It gave me strength and resolve. There were so many things that could go wrong during the race. I could forget my sequencing of movement or pull something. My hip might give out, or I might not have enough stamina. I could take a lot more than twenty-three steps now . . . but could I take enough for a mile? And if I failed, would I ever be an athlete? I knew that even if all of that happened, I had picked the right race to try walking in. My faith had taught me that with God all things are possible. I knew that even if I didn't make it, God had my back. Would *always* have my back.

Right then, I looked up and saw my walker. It was my turn.

THE HEART OF BATTLE

Dad took me out of the jogger and set my feet on either side of the PVC pipe on my walker.

He rested my elbows on the arm pads and tightened the black Velcro straps over my forearms and wrists. As he got me situated, people passing by us cheered me on. I smiled back at them and thanked them. I knew Mom, Annie, and Gracy were at the finish line, ready to commemorate the moment with photos and video.

"Okay, Johnny," Dad said. "You're ready."

Step, step, step, step. I started off flying! It seemed like there was an endless stream of runners and walkers encouraging me, and I tried to do the same for them. Father Mark found us and began to walk alongside.

"How ya doin', Johnny?"

"I sure feel better now that I have a priest walking beside me!"

Father Mark laughed and said, "Well good. I'm glad because I'm gonna stay with you until the finish if that's all right?"

"Sure! I love the company!"

Dad agreed, saying, "Yeah, maybe your steps will feel a little lighter now, Johnny!"

But all too soon my legs were heavy with fatigue, and I had started dragging my toe on each foot. I was having a hard time picking up my feet. I had been walking for about forty-five minutes and was almost halfway through the mile, but I was *tired*.

Dad forced me to take regular breaks so I could take a drink and catch my breath. But because I was getting so fatigued, I was losing my form. I was forgetting what I had to do, and the order in which I needed to do it. Over and over Dad reminded me to keep my head up and look forward. If my upper body stayed in the right position, I could shift my weight more easily *and* breathe more easily.

Even with the encouragement, I was slowing down considerably. Many of the runners who had already finished the 5K came back down the route to cheer me on. The clock kept ticking—and then I was the only one on the course.

I mean, I was the only one still *participating* in the 5K on the course. Some of the people who'd finished decided to walk beside me, retracing what they'd already finished.

"Go, Johnny, go!" a spectator hollered.

I forced myself to take a few more steps.

"You Can Do It!" a poster read.

I drew strength from the sign and took a few more steps.

"We're walking with you, Johnny," one of the finished runners would say.

Again, I'd force myself to take a few more steps. My community was giving me strength when I needed it most. Dad reminded me *again* to keep my head up. The moment I allowed it to tilt down, my whole body slumped forward. Then my toes would drag, my arms would shake, my breathing would get ragged. Trouble was, when I *did* look up, I got some bad news. We were closing in on the finish line, true, but I couldn't see it—because between the finish and me stood a hill. And if I was having this much trouble on the flat surface, I honestly didn't know if I could make it the final quarter mile.

Father Mark must have read my mind. "You can do it, Johnny Boy. It's more of a gentle slope, really!"

For the five hundredth time, I forced my head up and prayed for strength. I hoped Father Mark was right.

Meanwhile, Mom was worried. Just like the hill was blocking my view of the finish line, the hill was blocking Mom's view of me.

Just then, a friend came running up to her and said, "You *have* to go see what's happening!"

"Why? What's happening?" she asked nervously. "Is Johnny okay?"

"Don't worry, he's fine!" the friend assured her. "I mean, he's exhausted and out of breath . . . but what you'll see once you get over that hill will take your breath away!"

Along with Annie and Gracy, Mom walked quickly back down the route, and before long she could see down the slope of the hill.

The friend had been right: what she saw *did* take her breath away. Because by that time, the final tenth of a mile, there were *hundreds* of people walking beside and behind me.

Teens, children, moms pushing babies in strollers, dads holding toddlers on shoulders, race participants, parishioners . . . I had an *army* at my back. There were even elderly folks with folding chairs who were walking ahead, sitting down, cheering me on, and then standing up and carrying their chairs forward again. And there ahead of me—I could see her now—was Mom.

She told me later that the tears streaming down her face were for the absolute beauty of that moment. She said it was like the most important elements of goodness in the entire world had gathered in that one spot—and would stay for as long as I needed them.

I was surrounded by my family, one of the most important things in my life. I knew that my family would always be there for me. They had already proven that time and time again. They were there to lift me up and catch me when I fell, and they loved me unconditionally.

I was surrounded by my friends. Some I had known for a long time, and some I had just met on the course. But they were all there to encourage, help, and guide, giving me little grace-filled reminders that they were behind me, both literally and figuratively. They were laughing with me, sweating with me, and encouraging me. I felt completely surrounded by love. I could feel it all around me. It was like love had grown arms and hands, and was using them to pick up my feet when I felt like I couldn't take another step, patting my back and gently nudging me to keep moving, always present but never giving up. Love was living in the smiles and tears I saw as I journeyed up the road toward the finish.

And I was surrounded by my faith. The priest who walked beside me, gently reassuring me, serving as a subtle reminder to me that I was on the right path—not only in this race, but in life as well. As I neared the finish, I saw my faith in the gilded, cross-topped steeple that was catching the evening sun's light and shining in front of me in the distance. "Follow me," I felt it say, "and I will lead you to the finish . . . both in this race and in life."

Mom was right. Everything important to me in my world had gathered at that moment, with me, *for* me, and I found the strength and courage to continue.

Almost there. I had been dragging my feet so much that I had worn a hole in both toes of my shoes. My feet were burning, my eyes were stinging from the sweat, my stomach was cramping, my arms and hands ached from holding so tightly onto the walker, and my knees were tender from knocking against each other—but I never felt better in my entire life. I had more energy flowing through me than I had ever felt before. I knew I was going to achieve what I set out to do.

I could hear the race announcer ahead, and the music at the finish line, but I couldn't see the finish yet. And even in my beatdown, hyped-up state, the thought struck me. *I was walking by faith.* None of us can see where we will end up in life. We need faith to reach our goals and our final destination. We can't see it until we arrive. That's what faith is all about.

And then I reached the finish line.

All the training I had done, and the support I had received, had pushed me to this point. More people were waiting for me at the finish, cheering me on. I stepped across the timing strip and let go of the walker—and Dad caught me before I fell.

He was always doing that.

I raised my arms to the heavens as best I could, just like I'd seen other athletes do. The cheering got so loud! Achieving this had been worth every struggle, every ache, every pain. I kept my arms up as long as I could, and then I let them drop. I let my dad put me back into my jogger. And I hugged my mom and sisters tightly.

PRETTY DOGGONE GOOD

Unbeknownst to us, someone from our church had contacted our local news station, WOOD TV8, to let them know about my marathon mile, my impossible mile. When sports reporter Casey Jones arrived in a suit and tie, he thought he'd only stay a few minutes to grab some footage. But he was so moved by what was happening down the road that he ended up peeling off his suit coat and tie, rolling up his sleeves, and staying there to film everything. What was going to be a fifteen-minute shot turned out to be a couple of hours of capturing the emotion and thrill of that moment, both for me and our tight-knit community. What was going to be a short clip of the race ended up being two segments on the five, six, and eleven o'clock news.

Once things settled down, Coach Woj found me. I was a sweaty, sticky, stinking mess, but wore a huge smile on my face.

"Well, Johnny," he asked, "how'd it feel?"

"Coach, I just did what a lot of new runners do, I came out of the gate too fast! I was so excited to get going that I forgot to pace myself, which made me lose a lot of steam at the end. It was tough!"

"But you made it!" he said. "Now, next time, you learn from that lesson and make sure you pace yourself from the start. Get some chocolate milk to drink to help rebuild and replenish those muscles with protein. They were working hard today!"

"Will do, Coach!" I grinned.

His words were music to my ears. See, Coach had been telling *me* to replenish *my* muscles. Which meant . . . I was an athlete. It was the first time I had ever talked to a coach about my own experience, rather than something I saw or something Dad had gone through.

It was so surreal, such an incredible moment, that I was afraid I was dreaming, and I quickly prayed that it was real. If I had a dollar for every high-five I gave someone, or every picture I took, I could have bought myself ten cases of chocolate milk.

One gray-haired gentleman with glasses approached me. It took him awhile to work up to what he wanted to say. "Johnny, I heard you were walking in this race," he managed to say at last. "I just wanted to tell you that I had been feeling kind of down, and hearing that you were going to be walking in this race gave me a new perspective."

He placed his right leg up on the jogger next to me, then pulled up his pant leg, revealing a prosthetic leg.

"I walked in this race," he said, "because of you."

I didn't know what to say. I had no idea my decision to walk would affect him or any others. I was just out there to prove to myself that I could do something. That I could be someone I had always wanted to be, an athlete like my dad. It was my way of thanking Dad for all he had done for me. I didn't know I could have this kind of impact on someone, and I felt so humbled and happy.

"Thank you!" I said. "I'm glad I got you out there! How'd it feel?"

"Pretty doggone good, Johnny. Pretty doggone good." We smiled, both knowing full well what he meant.

The day after the St. Patrick 5K, I made it into Father Mark's sermon. He stood at the front of the sanctuary, dressed as always in his vestments and wearing a smile. Summer light poured in through the stained glass windows. There was a happy buzz in the room after the excitement of the parish festival weekend.

"I know many of you were here last night, when our own Johnny Agar completed his race," he began. It seemed like almost everyone smiled and nodded their heads. *I wasn't just an athlete now,* I joked to myself, *I was closer in getting to Heaven after being in a sermon!*

Father then talked about how he'd noticed something during the race: that when I kept my head up and stayed focused on the road in front of me, I walked better and straighter. But as soon as I put my head down, my whole body started to collapse, which made it far more difficult for me to keep moving forward.

"That's the way we all need to look at our faith journeys," he told us, looking from face to face. "We all need to journey with our heads up, and our eyes focused on the goal . . . just like Johnny."

PART III

The Road to Achieving

CHAPTER 11

[The Successful Failure]

My life was filled with improbabilities. I am not blind to the fact that being born with cerebral palsy automatically made me the underdog. My diagnosis handed me a postmarked, dated, and signed letter from the world telling me I was "not normal." Fortunately, I learned how to tear letters like that up with every challenge I faced and every doubtful thought I had.

Most people would have said my fate was sealed being born with cerebral palsy, but my parents refused to believe that—and with the help of a kind doctor—they made a decision that would have a profound impact on my life.

Dr. Batton was a tall, broad man with blond hair and glasses. Mom said he had a very unassuming and calm presence about him that both she and Dad liked. When I was still a preemie in the NICU, they got called into his office. Looking at them through his gold-rimmed glasses, he gently said, "There is something I saw in Johnny's ultrasound that concerns us." Then he paused. "The ultrasound indicates to us that your son has cerebral palsy."

My parents said tears started to stream down both their faces—their plans for my future had just been drastically changed. And while they did not understand fully what cerebral palsy was at that point, they knew it was not good. The way they had envisioned their life as a family of three, they said, was going to resemble nothing like they had dreamed about years before. Before that day, they wondered if I would be interested in things like student leadership, running track, magic tricks, playing baseball—all the things they had participated in as kids.

Now they had to readjust their thinking because there was a new reality. They had a son with cerebral palsy.

Dad asked if I would be able to walk. Dr. Batton said it was highly unlikely based on where the bleed was in my brain. He thought all my limbs would be affected, as well as my speech.

Mom asked, "Will this have an effect on his understanding of things around him? Will he be able to understand his environment?" Dr. Batton couldn't give a definitive answer for that other than a time-will-tell response.

It had been pretty devastating news for them. They both wanted to know what books he would recommend so they could arm themselves with what to expect and how to treat me. Remember, this was 1994 when the internet was just an idea and hard-copy books were how people obtained information.

And this is when Dr. Batton helped change the course of my life.

He leaned forward in his seat and said to my parents, "I can give you all sorts of titles of books that can teach you everything you need to know about cerebral palsy, if you would like that. I can give you some of the books now, and you can take them with you when you leave this office, but can I make a suggestion?

"In all the years I have been practicing, I have seen a lot of parents come through those doors having to hear similar information. And I have seen a lot of those parents anticipate failures because of the knowledge they have regarding their child's specific diagnosis. But what I want to tell you is, you have a choice. You can leave this room and read as much as you want about cerebral palsy—its causes, its diagnosis, the risks involved, the different types, and the treatments and interventions for it—or you can love your son unconditionally and take life with him day by day, one step at a time, without worrying about what 'could happen.'

"I have found that a lot of the things you read may never happen, but you still anticipate them and tend to not push your child to do those things, or you wait for them to happen."

I am told that at that moment, my parents knew—they were sure, in fact—what choice they were going to make. They left that office without any books in their hands. They left with the knowledge that they were going to love me unconditionally and live life as they always had—with faith in God's plan for us, and a deep love for each other and for the newest member of their family, me.

The choice they made that day shaped who I am and the way I look at life today, because they treated me as their son, instead of their son with cerebral palsy.

WORLDWIDE LEADER IN SPORTS

When I sleep, I don't dream very much. Maybe it's because I do a lot of daydreaming when I'm awake and my mind just wants to rest when I'm asleep. I'm not sure. But there was one morning I woke up, and I was disheartened to find out I wasn't the major league pitcher I had just dreamed I was.

I had been out on the mound and was one batter away from a no-hitter. My catcher called for a fastball on the inside. Strike one! The next call, a curve. I shook it off. *No way*, I thought, *he would expect that now. Let's put a little more heat on it.* I threw a fastball to the outside corner. Ball! The batter dug his feet in closer to the plate. I was getting to him. Next, I threw a fastball down the gut—swing and a miss. Strike two! The batter stepped out of the box again, adjusted his glove straps and his helmet—a ritual he liked to do. He was nervous. *Good,* I thought. *Let me see if I can throw you even more off balance.*

The crowd was going wild, chanting my name. I was one pitch away from my no-hitter. I knew my team behind me was ready for anything—they had my back. The next pitch I threw was a breaking ball. Strike three! The team charged at me, patting me on the back and lifting me up to celebrate. They kept me up there so long, my legs started cramping and became tight . . . and then I woke up realizing the cramps and tightness in my legs were *real*. My body was reminding me it was only a delusion.

Dreams are really remarkable because you can move your body any way it wants to go. It was one of those dreams where you wish you could fall back to sleep in order to keep it going.

I'm fortunate because my cerebral palsy gives me a lot of time to reflect on things. It seems my inability to "always be on the go" gives me that advantage. I have more time to recreate, imagine, and dream. That's why I was scared that some news I had just received was not really real. I feared I was only dreaming it too . . .

I had been at the Conductive Learning Center for more than fifteen years now and had made some lifelong friends. The growth of the program had started a degreed program that trained Aquinas students to become conductors upon graduation. I became very good friends with all of the student-teachers, but there was one my family and I especially became good friends with—Clare Avery.

After I had walked at the St. Patrick 5K, and knowing how much I loved everything having to do with sports, Clare decided to call ESPN to let them know about my one-mile walk. I had no idea she was attempting to call—she didn't tell me in case nothing came of it. I was quite familiar with all the shows on ESPN, since Annie and I both aspired to work there one day. When Mom handed me the phone one July morning, saying it was the executive producer of *E:60*, a prime-time sports magazine show, I knew exactly what show she was talking about. I just had no clue why they would be calling me.

"Hi, Johnny, this is Andy Tennant. I'm the executive producer for ESPN's *E:60* show. Have you heard of it?"

"Absolutely! My sister and I watch it all the time!" I excitedly answered.

Mr. Tennant went on, "Well, a friend of yours, Clare Avery, contacted me and told me about your one-mile walk! Congratulations!"

"Oh, thank you so much! I appreciate that!"

"I also saw the local footage that your news station captured and wanted to know if you wouldn't mind if we featured you on *E:60*?"

Was this a dream? No, my legs were kicking with excitement as I began to slide off the couch. No, this was real!

"What?! I would be honored!" I shouted. "Thank you so much! Oh, my goodness!"

I had fallen off the couch by this time. Mom and Dad had given up trying to keep me on it. The conversation continued on the floor, where they were now trying to prevent me from dropping the phone.

"Great! I will be in touch within the next couple of weeks to let you know when we can send a crew out to your house to film you and your family, but in the meantime, keep working hard."

"Will do! Thank you so much again, Mr. Tennant. I can't believe this and am so excited for the opportunity!"

I hung up the phone and screamed with pure elation. Even though Annie and Gracy really had no idea what was happening yet, they were excited because I was excited.

The producer, Matt Rissmiller, and his film crew came to our house toward the end of fall to film. They were going to follow us throughout our daily routine to show viewers what my life was like. Dad and I had already signed up for the 2013 Mitchell's Run and the Ludington Triathlon, which were back to back, so the crew made plans to be at both events. We also learned that famed journalist and news reporter Bob Woodruff was going to conduct the interviews at our house.

The next morning, the film crew arrived at our house and began to unload their vehicle, bringing out huge cameras, cables, lights, and all sorts of cases. Seeing them arrive with all of the equipment brought reality to the forefront for us. It was all so hard to believe that ESPN was at our house—and wanted to film *us*! For our sports-loving family, having the biggest sports network in the world at our house was pretty awesome.

During the Mitchell's Run, they placed several GoPro cameras on my walker and had a cameraman on a golf cart to get some good shots of us while we were running. They also put portable microphones on all of us, so they could capture our responses the moment I walked across the finish line. However, I don't think they planned on capturing as much as they did with those mics! We had been wearing them for most of the day, forgetting they were even attached to us.

Prior to the race, I had to use the bathroom. Maybe it was nerves, maybe I really did have to go, but whatever the case, I was having a hard time going. Usually, if I was able to relax by laughing, I could go with no problem, so my parents were both trying to get me to laugh by making up songs to sing or telling corny jokes about the day. We all had completely forgotten we were still mic'd up, until we came out of the bathroom and saw Matt and the sound guy smiling profusely.

While we were in the van following Matt, Dad made the comment that he forgot to get Matt's cell phone number. Annie, sitting in the backseat thinking about Matt—who looked like he had just walked off the set of a *GQ* photo shoot—leaned forward and said, "Oh, *I'll* get Matt's number for you!" We all looked at her and signaled to her to stop—her mic was still on. I had never seen her face turn that many shades of red before. She tried to recover by saying, ". . . So that I can give his number to you, Dad," but we were laughing so hard by then it didn't matter anymore.

As usual, Mitchell's Run brought in a lot of participants on race day. The streets were crowded with people, and I was so happy ESPN was able to film me walking in this race. It was our hometown race. It was where I grew up, and where all my friends were.

My walking was extremely strained, but the last quarter of a mile took the runners right through the downtown area where the streets were lined with people shaking cowbells and cheering on the participants. As I turned the corner in the last stretch, I was amazed to see how many people were there. Their words of encouragement lifted my body up, making me feel as though I could do anything, including reaching that finish line. I had always heard athletes talking about being motivated by the crowd, now I understood what that meant.

Those last few steps, Dad helped me push my walker. It was a familiar scene. Not the fact that I had him push my walker when I walked, but that Dad was behind me, nudging me along. It was a space he had occupied my entire life. He had always been there for me whenever I needed him for anything. This moment, this race, this time in my life was not foreign; it was no different. Dad was there not to control my walker but just as a reassuring hand, guiding, assisting, helping to push it along—me along—and to remind me that although I had to do the work, he would always be there to catch me if I fell.

I made it across the finish line to cheers of excitement and tears of joy—mostly all from Mom, who had walked beside me the whole way. She had known how much that moment had meant to me; every moment I was given an opportunity to be the athlete I had always dreamed about becoming.

Mom said when I crossed that finish line, she immediately thought about all the surgeries and therapies, and the struggles I had gone through. How the doctors had told them I probably would never walk or be able to talk and were even unsure how much of the world I would comprehend. It overwhelmed her with happiness to realize all of those negatives in my life, all those unknowns, had led me to this moment.

I remember being asked right when I crossed the finish line, what it felt like for me to walk across it on my own two feet. I imagined what I was feeling was similar to what a baseball player felt when he hit one out of the park, or how a hockey player felt when he swept one cleanly into the net, or how a football player felt when doing a touchdown celebration dance in the end zone.

I imagined I felt like an athlete.

When I was about eight years old, I remember crawling up to the window to look out at some neighborhood kids playing a game of baseball in our cul-de-sac. Mom saw me watching and came up to me.

"Penny for your thoughts, Buddy?" Mom said.

I was silent, just watching and listening to the fun they were having.

"Johnny," Mom stroked my hair, "does it bother you not to be able to walk or do things quite like the other kids can?" She had never asked me that question before.

I looked out at the kids playing and then answered her honestly. "Sometimes, Mom. But I know God has a plan for me . . . I just have to wait and see what that is."

Now, after working hard to cross the finish line, I thought that maybe all those times I just sat there, yearning and dreaming, fueled me and led me to this moment at Mitchell's Run. Maybe this was part of God's plan for me.

I looked at the reporter standing in front of me at the finish, and through my breathlessness, I replied, "Before I did a race with my dad, I would always participate. But now that I crossed . . . it feels like I am officially an athlete."

I knew I could do anything I set out to accomplish. I struggled and wanted to give up several times during that walk, but I didn't.

TAKING CONTROL

It took me one hour and forty-five minutes to walk that mile at the St. Patrick 5K back in 2013, but it really took me nineteen years. Nineteen years of surgeries, comments, and looks. Of gazing in the mirror at the person I was and realizing I wasn't as independent as I thought I had been. Forcing me to realize that I had to fight my disability on my own to reach my goals. I knew I had been given the tools and the guidance by my family, but now it was up to me. To take control of my body instead of it controlling me.

That one idea to walk a mile was an opportunity for me to spread my wings like the butterfly I had watched and cared for when I was little. I knew my "flight" may be awkward and slow, but I had the opportunity to fly, and I spread my wings as far as they could go to catch the wind.

It all culminated in that one-mile walk. I had done it. I proved to myself and to all those who doubted me that I could do it. But as I had repeatedly been reminded, failure is always right around the corner, waiting.

SOMETIMES YOU WIN, SOMETIMES YOU LEARN

Known as the biggest and most brutal one-day endurance event in the world, the Ironman World Championship is held every year in Kona, Hawaii. The "Super Bowl of triathlons" consists of a 2.4-mile swim, a 112-mile bike ride, and a 26.2-mile run. In order to compete in the race, you have to get a qualifying time in another Ironman race. There is also a physically challenged athlete division, and, for that, you put your name in a lottery from which five names are drawn.

One day in the spring of 2016, a friend of ours called to see if Dad and I would be interested in participating in it. That year, it was on October 8.

"Do you think Johnny and Jeff would be up to it?" he asked Mom.

"I'm not sure?" Mom said, looking at me nodding my head yes because I could hear the conversation. "Johnny would do it in a heartbeat. He is sitting right here already telling me he wants to submit their names, but we have to ask Jeff."

When she got off the phone, she told me not to get my hopes up. Dad had never done a full-distance Ironman race with me yet, and he would *never* swim in the ocean. He hated the thought of sharks and other sea creatures swimming underneath him.

That night, at dinner, Mom let him know about the phone call from our friend.

"So, what do you think?" she asked with hesitation.

Dad looked at me first. I was smiling broadly. Then he turned to Mom and said, "I think we should give it a shot. Right, Johnny?!"

Mom's mouth hung wide open. "But you don't like swimming in the ocean! You have never done a full-distance Ironman! How are you going to do that?"

I chimed in quickly, "Mom, you and Dad have always told me never to back down from something just because it's difficult or because I was scared of failing. You guys have always told me not to let my fears hold me back."

Mom knew what I said was true. How could she stop us when my whole life she had taught me to never be afraid of trying? Dad knew it, too; that's why he was ready to do what he could to practice what he had preached for so many years.

It was several weeks later when we received an email from Ironman—we had been chosen to go to Kona. We had six months to prepare. It was game time.

There was so much to do, and we immediately got to work. Dad started training with a local coach to get race ready. He woke up at 4:00 a.m. to swim or bike for two hours, and then he went to work until six or seven at night. In the evening, he trained more by biking, running, or weightlifting. His days sometimes lasted until midnight.

Mom started working on getting sponsorships to offset the cost to get us to Hawaii. She was able to secure several sponsors that generously helped with money and equipment. I was happy to say my alma mater came through for me as well. In addition to donating money, Aquinas College dedicated the Aquinas 5K run to TeamAgar. They made it a Hawaiian-themed run, complete with leis, and donated most of the proceeds to our race efforts in Kona. The whole Aquinas basketball team came out to participate, lining up to high-five me before the start of the race. It was an unbelievably kind gesture, and we were so thankful and humbled by the support we received.

As for my part, I started training a lot more, too, so I would be ready to walk the last mile. Since Dad's time was consumed, we were finding it difficult to get in the right amount of training time I needed to walk. There just weren't enough hours in the day. Mom tried to pick up the slack by taking me out on some training walks, but watching me struggle, sweat, and breathe heavily proved to be too difficult for her. Her nurturing side would take over, which made it difficult for me to push myself when she was asking me constantly if I needed to stop to take a break.

There are some people who come into your life and make it infinitely better just by being in their sphere. I am lucky enough to have two such people: my mom's cousin Chris Doucette, whom I call Uncle Chris, and his wife, Janet. Aunt Janet stands all of four foot nine, but every inch of her is packed with the best of everything that is good in this world. I think when God made her, He filled her with so much love and kindness that He knew she didn't need to be any taller—her small frame clearly had enough for a thousand lifetimes. Uncle Chris is the most caring and gentle soul I know. He's always willing to lend a hand or be there when I need him. You know those people who will drop everything they are doing to come and help someone in need? That describes these two. I have never met two people who have more kindness. Like a swollen river breaching a levy, their goodness overflows in abundance reaching out to their three daughters, Emily, Mary, and Lily as well.

Aunt Janet and Uncle Chris stepped in to help me with my training walks. They offered to walk with me a few times a week. Aunt Janet is an occupational therapist, which was a bonus in helping me to keep my muscles stretched. They were always pushing me to do better, go a little farther, or improve my time.

To conquer my dad's fear and inexperience of swimming in the ocean, Chad Spaman, our friend from myTeam Triumph who lived in Oceanside, California, offered to have Dad out for some practice swims in the Pacific, which was only a block from his house. It was perfect for Dad to get up every morning and go for a swim.

The first thing Dad noticed was the increased buoyancy because of the salt water. The second was the stingrays that sometimes lay on the ocean floor underneath him. "Shuffle your feet when you walk out into the water," Chad told Dad, "that way the stingrays will stay clear of your feet."

At one point, he and Chad were a mile offshore when something huge swam underneath them. Dad was a little freaked out, but Chad reassured him, "Don't worry, it's just a giant manta ray."

"Oh, that's all?!" Dad muttered sarcastically.

By the time Dad left, he had a pretty good grasp on what it was like swimming in the ocean. The next order of business was to line up the equipment we were going to need. Terence, who had competed in several Ironmans, said we could borrow one of myTeam Triumph's boats. Dad and I had used one during the other triathlons we had done together, and we were both familiar with how it behaved in the water.

In prepping to get the right bike, Dad was introduced to a world champion duathlete named Fred Bunn. Fred knew a lot about road bikes and graciously offered to meet up with us to take a look at Dad's bike. The Kona race was a different animal, and Dad wasn't sure his clearance-rack bike would work.

Dad asked, "Well, what are your thoughts, Fred?" Dad was ready for some sage advice.

To have a good laugh, Fred put his hand up to his chin. "Well, here's the first thing you should do. You should first take those cute little reflectors off your wheels, so you actually look like a cyclist!"

We thought Fred had his hand up to his mouth in contemplation, but he was actually trying to conceal his laughter. Not missing a beat, Dad countered, "Yeah, I took the basket and bell off the handlebars yesterday and forgot about the reflectors . . ."

When all the joking was done, Dad said it was at that point when he realized we may have been in way over our heads.

FOR ME

Sometimes ignorance truly is bliss. We had no idea what a big undertaking the Ironman World Championship was going to be when we first decided to participate—and that was a blessing. At this point, there was no way Dad was going to back down—it wasn't in his DNA. There was also no way my parents were going to say no when they had been telling me my whole life to say yes to every challenge I faced. They weren't going to let an opportunity for me to participate in the Super Bowl of triathlons pass by, when all I ever wanted was to be an athlete. I realized they had taken a huge leap of faith, and that they were doing it all for me.

Dad never cared if he was called an Ironman. He wanted *me* to be called the Ironman. I was very aware of—and incredibly thankful for—what he was doing for me. I watched every day as he put his body through grueling workouts, coming into the room with a shirt that was dripping wet with sweat, as if he had just jumped in a pool with it on, or moving slowly because his muscles ached from the previous night of weightlifting.

I would hear him come in the door as I was just waking up, having already run ten or more miles on the indoor track at the Y. I listened to him trail off to sleep midsentence while talking with Mom because he was too exhausted to think anymore. I watched how he studied the experts, talked to people, and agonized over how to get through the race one hour early so I would have enough time to walk across the finish line.

I could almost taste how badly he wanted this—but not for him—for me. Most importantly, I could feel the love he had for me. It was in every drop of sweat, every ice pack or heating pad, every pound lost, every workout, every ache, every sore muscle, and every smile he conjured up for me when he finished his workout for the day. He was showing the love of a father to his son, and I knew I was extremely blessed to have him as my dad.

STEPPING-STONES

I can't begin to explain the beauty that is Hawaii. It was hard to believe that this island would turn into an adversary for so many triathletes. The beauty and grandeur we were seeing along the Queen Ka'ahumanu Highway would soon be passed quickly by bikers and runners who needed to stay focused on the road ahead of them. The beautiful black rock would not be regaled for its different shapes and unusual textures, but rather be cursed because of the heat it captured and sent back out to the participants along the Kona coast. The tropical breeze, which was welcomed for its cooling effect, would be under contempt for its crosswind strength of up to forty miles per hour, sometimes blowing the bikes off the course. The magnificent expanse of ocean with its cool waters and calming wave effect would be met with anxiety and distress as the weather wreaks havoc on its unpredictable wave formation and potentially strong currents for the swimmers.

It was hard to say what all of that would be like on race day for Dad and me, but the day to find out was finally here. To add to the excitement, NBC was filming us on our journey for its Ironman World Championship Kona preview show. If we succeeded or failed, it would be at an international level. No pressure, right?

We all said a prayer for safety, calm waters, the wind to be behind our backs, and for us to feel lifted during the run. We also prayed that we could have a positive influence on someone in the process of this race-day opportunity.

Dad and I had a good swim and made it in the time—one hour and fifty minutes—we were shooting for, despite the dramatic change in conditions halfway through the swim. The winds kicked up and pushed the boat so hard that it was perpendicular to Dad and would pull him backward. Dad used almost all of the energy he had just to get back to shore on the return leg. We had made it through the first 2.4 miles.

Once we transitioned, we were out onto the bike course, but unfortunately, we were unable to make the cutoff time. We had made it halfway through—56 miles—and they had to pull us from the course. Our race was over.

Dad never gave up. I watched his legs and his body work extremely hard, pumping the pedals to get me closer and closer to the finish line, but it just wasn't our day. It was a somber moment for both of us. Failure is a hard pill to swallow. I had been on top of the world after walking my impossible mile, yet here I was at the bottom again. I was thinking about my favorite athletes and how they bounced back from losses, how they were able to get themselves back up again, and how much more I respected them now.

When they took us off the course, the driver who was going to take us back to our hotel came over and shook our hands. He said he was sorry we didn't make it this time. I responded, "Sometimes you win, sometimes you learn."

Failure was teaching me again.

My whole life I had learned that failure was a process, not an end; that the challenges you face are just stepping-stones, not roadblocks. I needed something good to come out of the bad, or my attempts felt futile. It was the way I had been able to stretch my imagination outside the borders of my restricted body to see a brighter future for me.

The odds were against us in this race. Yet, we still weren't afraid to try. And, man, did we give it our all. Dad had taught me never to let my fears hold me back. He was still teaching me that at that moment, and I was still willing to learn.

I learned that success isn't just the medal you show at the end of the race, it's the mettle you show at the start of the race too.

Our whole TeamAgar crew was there at the hotel waiting for us: Mom, Annie, Gracy, Terence, Aunt Janet, Uncle Chris, and my cousins Emily, Mary, and Lily. Very few words were said, but love didn't need words. We knew what they wanted to say; they said it with their hugs, their help, and their relentless support.

CHAPTER 12

[Dreamer]

I knew that not finishing Kona was part of God's bigger plan. I always wondered, though, why God couldn't have taken the day off that day? I didn't have to wait too long before I realized why. My successes *and* my failures were about to grant me a beautiful gift in the form of champions.

I remember watching Justin Verlander play when I was nine years old. He was pitching for the US national team in the Pan American Games. They earned a silver medal. He was a great pitcher even back then, but it wasn't just his pitching I admired. I tried to model my life by the way he commanded the game. A Detroit Tiger for thirteen years, he never backed down, and if he failed, he learned from it and either got better or moved on. He was mentally tough and seemed to become stronger when faced with any kind of challenge. His tenacity and willingness to overcome difficult situations really showed me how to face my own challenges. I knew he also was close to his dad. I studied everything about him and couldn't help but make him a larger-than-life figure.

At one point in his career, he underwent rehab after a surgery. He had always been tough, and I knew he would come back to pitch stronger than ever. While he was rehabbing, he was watching ESPN—and the *E:60* show with me came on. Motivated by my perseverance, and noticing I was wearing his Tigers jersey in one of the shots, he invited my family and me to watch a game in his suite as his guest. I thought I had died and gone to Heaven.

When we arrived at Comerica Park, home of the Detroit Tigers, we were met by Jordan Field, director of community relations and head of the Detroit Tigers Foundation. Jordan led my whole family, including my grandpa, out to the field to watch batting practice and to meet Justin.

There were quite a few people on the field with us, most of whom were the press. Verlander was about thirty feet from us and was surrounded by reporters and cameras. As I looked at the field, I imagined what it must be like to stand out on the mound with the stadium full, and face opponent after opponent, giving it your all every time you threw a pitch. I had a newfound respect for Verlander. It's one thing to see him pitch on TV, but it's a totally different viewpoint when you're standing on the field—in his office—taking in the sights and sounds from down on the grass. The enormity of the pressure he had to experience was incredible: the bevy of people vying for his attention, the gravity of making sure he says and does the right thing, the massiveness of the stadium against the small little pitching mound, the TV cameras set up all around the field, and the amount of activity going on both inside and out to prepare for a baseball game—his game.

Suddenly there was some movement to our left. Reporters and cameras started parting to reveal Verlander walking toward us. He came directly to me and held out his hand, shaking mine.

"Johnny, how's it goin', man?"

"Hi, Justin, how ya' doin', buddy?"

"You were a real inspiration for me," he said. "That was awesome."

It was hard for me to grasp. The guy who had won the Cy Young Award and MVP, the guy who was an American League strikeout leader, and the guy who I thought pitched a lot like I had to handle life—constantly making adjustments to adapt—said I was an inspiration to him? If this was a dream, I never wanted to be awakened.

I had thought about this moment and knew what I wanted to say: "I just want to thank you for showing me how to handle tough situations that sometimes get thrown at us. I really admire how when the game gets tougher for you, like in life, you get tougher, and that has shown me how I need to be. Thank you for that."

Verlander's eyes became moist. He later said to reporters that I had struck a chord in his heart. It was a pretty special moment for both of us.

After we chatted some more and got some pictures together, we went up to Verlander's suite, located high above the field between home plate and third base. It was about the height my feet were floating after having such an incredible day that I would never forget.

Maybe I looked up to athletes so much because I looked up to my dad so much. He was the athlete who taught me the most. Those other athletes were there for me when I looked for them, but my dad? He was there for me every day, guiding me every step of the way, even when he wasn't guiding me. I watched and learned from him. We were living life, but he was always there teaching, encouraging, helping.

In the winter, he was there pulling me on a sled while cross-country skiing, and when spring came along, it was baseball season and time to show me how to place my crooked fingers on the seam of the ball to throw the perfect curve. In the summer, we went on long, slow boat rides around the lake, talking about nothing special but everything important, and fall brought football games and tailgating. He wanted to know how my day went, what the best part had been, and what I hoped to be when I grew up. What I really wanted to be was just like my dad—an athlete whom I looked up to every day of my life.

Agar, Verlander, Shanahan, Smoltz, Yzerman, Jordan. They were all athletes I had relied on to get me through challenging times—but there was another great athlete who inspired me.

G.O.A.T.

Every Olympics, both summer and winter games, we decorated the living room with flags, posters with the Olympics logo on them, and red, white, and blue streamers. We even had pseudo-gold medals that our parents gave out when we did something gold medal-worthy, like cleaning without being asked. We knew the Olympics were a big deal because we never got to eat dinner around the TV, but when the games were on, we sat on the floor at the coffee table to watch the competitions. And we got to stay up past our bedtime.

I remember the 2004 Athens Olympics like it was yesterday. I was ten years old when Phelps took the block and won his first gold medal in the four-hundred-meter medley. He was why I was so glued to the TV. Not because NBC commentator Bob Costas and others had predicted he would win a gold, but because of what I heard him say before the Olympics even started: "I think if you really just have a wide-open mind and use your imagination, I think a lot of things are possible."

I remember thinking I wanted him to be right. And when he won that first gold medal that day and broke his own world record doing it, he had proven it to me—that if I worked hard and kept dreaming, I could achieve anything. He had given me hope.

Now, thirteen years later, Dad and I were training for another Ironman—the Ironman 70.3 Florida—so I enveloped myself in positivity to help motivate me. Here I was, turning to Phelps for support again. Under Armour, an athletic apparel brand, had produced a commercial with Phelps called "Rule Yourself." The tagline, "It's what you do in the dark that puts you in the light," haunted me and reminded me that life was not easy, but that if you worked hard and stayed determined, you could reach your goal. I watched that commercial repeatedly to help motivate me to keep going. I wanted to get back to Kona with Dad eventually, and watching that video, I thought, was like my yellow brick road leading me there.

Phelps inspired me, not just because of his talent and all his gold medals, but because he had also risen, fallen, and risen again. The athletes whom my parents had encouraged me to emulate were not the ones who were always on top. They were the ones who had experienced failure and yet were able to rise again, who had made their way back up to the top victorious— not defeated.

Phelps's athletic life had provided the extra "push" when I needed it most. I didn't watch or follow him because I was a young aspiring swimmer looking to perfect my freestyle stroke like his. A lot of people say I kind of looked like him, but I knew I definitely didn't swim like him! I had a *no*-style stroke and was just happy to be able to kick my legs enough that I didn't drown in the process. I followed him because of his work ethic, his mental toughness, and his attitude that showed me anything was possible.

That minute-and-a-half spot fired me up so much that Mom made the same "commercial" but replaced Phelps's swimming with my walking. We then uploaded it to YouTube.

FAILURE BRINGS ABOUT OPPORTUNITY

We had arrived in Florida a few days before the race, so we could make a trip out to Disney World. We were on a bus to one of the parks when Mom's phone rang.

It was Michael Phelps.

The video Mom made had reached him. We got off the bus and Mom handed me the phone.

"This is Johnny Agar," I said.

"Hi, Johnny, it's Michael Phelps."

"Oh, my goodness, how are you, buddy?! It's good to hear from you!"

"I wanted to call and wish you the best of luck at the Ironman in a few days. Nicole and I will be cheering you on from Arizona."

"Thank you so much! That means so much to me!"

"Just keep trying to think about your goals and your dreams, and if you work hard enough anything is possible, right? We want you to accomplish every goal you have, and there's not a doubt in my mind that you can do it."

That sentence choked me up. Trying to gain my composure, I responded, "That's one of the things you have taught me . . . throughout your training and all the hard times you have gone through. It really inspires me to do my best," I said to him.

"You can achieve anything you want to achieve, Johnny. Remember that."

If we had thought it was suffocatingly hot and humid in Florida before, it was really hard to breathe now. I was completely speechless after his call, but so, so very ready to take on an Ironman. The greatest Olympian of all time had just given me a pep talk—and I gulped down the optimism he was serving.

About two days later, Mom got another phone call. This time it was from an executive at Under Armour wishing us luck. We received a gift the next day: a package of Under Armour gear for each of us. While we loved the clothes, I thought the best part was the note that laid underneath all of the duffel bags. It was a note that wished us luck and was signed, "From your Under Armour Family."

With great coaching, along with encouragement from Michael Phelps and Under Armour, Dad and I finished in seven hours and forty minutes, beating our predicted time by five minutes. This was a huge victory for us on that Sunday in 2017.

"SURPRISE!"

Our partnership with our new coaches started when Aunt Janet and Uncle Chris met Thad Beaty and Nicole Serraiocco first in 2016 at the Los Angeles airport—then we saw them again at the practice swim in Kona, then again at a grocery store in Hawaii, then again in a store in New York City. They knew all those chance meetings were put there for a reason, and they wanted to help us with a shot at getting back to Kona—so they took us on as two of their athletes. Nicole was a certified coach with a huge heart. She had taken on an Ironman and decided to help others do the same. Thad was the lead guitarist for the country superstar band Sugarland. The touring lifestyle, coupled with a health scare with his mom, led him to take control of his health, becoming a certified coach. They were both extremely knowledgeable about training and what it was going to take for us to be successful.

Dad and I were a challenge for them. Dad was not just training as a two-hundred-pound athlete; when pulling the gear and me, it was like training as a three-hundred-fifty-pound athlete. So, they reevaluated all of our equipment needs, including getting us a more aerodynamic boat. According to Thad, ours looked like we had been using "the lovechild of the *Titanic* and a boat that stormed the beaches of Normandy." They had helped us train for—and finish—the Ironman in Florida, and now we were focused on Kona.

About two weeks later, Thad and Nicole called my mom to tell her some big news. Under Armour was going to turn my "Rule Yourself" video into a commercial, and they wanted to premiere it at a surprise party for Dad and me in our hometown. Over several days, Mom worked covertly to help with the plans, including Under Armour's request for inviting two hundred of our closest friends and family to help us celebrate.

Under Armour had contacted Verlander, and he graciously taped a message to me that was to play before the commercial. They had also contacted the local media and set up an area in the restaurant where the *Today* show could interview Dad and me.

Mom arranged a way to get us there so we would still be completely in the dark about everything. When we got to the venue and the elevator doors opened, standing there in front of me was a wall of our friends and family wearing TeamAgar shirts that read, "Sometimes You Win, Sometimes You Learn." They waved TeamAgar pennants and yelled, "Surprise!"

I popped my seatbelt right off from my wheelchair and started to slide down onto the elevator floor with excitement. As I wheeled through the crowd of almost 350 people, I began to get emotional. All these people had been there for me at some stage throughout my life. They had believed in me, helped me, pushed me, cried with me, and laughed with me—I was so very blessed and so very grateful. The TeamAgar shirts didn't represent just Dad and me as the team; everyone standing around us right then—they were all part of TeamAgar.

One of the Under Armour execs took the microphone. "Johnny's story is so compelling because it embodies the Under Armour spirit, and we wanted to share that with as many people as we could. So, we have made Johnny's 'Rule Yourself' video into a commercial, and it will be making its debut here in just a few minutes during his favorite team's game—the Detroit Tigers. But before that happens, there is someone special to Johnny who wanted to say something to him first."

Just then, the TV screens mounted around the room came on, and Verlander started talking: "Johnny, dude, your own ad! How cool! You're going to be the most famous Under Armour athlete yet. I hope you guys have a great time tonight!"

Wow. Under Armour really knew how to throw a party! The Tigers game started, and I chatted with as many people as

I possibly could. The crowd suddenly quieted down; it was the first commercial break. The screen went black, and words slowly appeared on the screen:

In March 2017, an athlete from Michigan recreated an Under Armour commercial featuring Michael Phelps. In celebration of Johnny, we are proud to bring you his film.

And then they played my commercial.

Sometimes you are lucky enough to see things from every direction. As I watched that video, I realized how happy I was at all the setbacks I had experienced in my life. The failures that I had gone through time and time again. The embarrassment. The rejection. The uncertainties. Those failures are what brought me to this place. Where I was sitting right now. Watching myself on TV, side by side with Michael Phelps, the greatest Olympian ever.

I was grateful that I had parents who taught me to never give up. Who showed me that we all were different—it was what made us all special. Parents who showed me the importance of humor and what it means to believe in something even when you can't see it, feel it, or grab it in your hands and hold onto it tightly. I was glad I had tried. I was glad I had put one foot in front of the other—literally and figuratively. It brought me to this moment. This wonderful, amazing moment.

I didn't want the night to end, but I knew it was inevitable. On the way home, I asked Dad if we had dreamed the whole thing. Dad said he wasn't sure, but if so, it was the best dream he had ever had. I agreed.

A few months later in August, Dad and I competed in the Ironman 70.3 Boulder in Colorado. It was my first time walking across the finish line at an Ironman competition, and I did it while the race speakers played Journey's "Don't Stop Believin'." I thought it was the most perfect and fitting song.

AMBASSADOR

Under Armour had invited us to come to their corporate headquarters in Baltimore, Maryland, about two months later. They wanted to give us a tour of their facilities and had asked if I could speak at their companywide Teammate Talk. It's not every day you can speak to such a huge and reputable company like Under Armour. Part of the tour led us down a long, dark corridor. As I wheeled down, I began to see a huge screen that was occupied entirely by my face wearing an Under Armour hat. Two gentlemen emerged from around the corner to introduce themselves.

"Hi, I'm Kevin McDermond," one said as he held out his hand, "and this is Ryan Rossi."

They shook our hands and led us to some black leather chairs stitched with the UA logo. As we sat, Kevin and Ryan explained that this big wall made up of individual screens was called the Make You Famous wall. Every Under Armour athlete who visits gets a personalized presentation of their life. It was hard to believe this was really happening to me. I was an Under Armour ambassador.

As my presentation started, Kevin and Ryan recounted my life—beginning with when I was a preemie and leading all the way up to when I had crossed the finish line at the Ironman 70.3 Boulder just weeks ago.

"Johnny," Kevin said, "I want you to know, when we put that video out on our social media sites, it was one of the top-performing pieces we had ever had. You ranked right up there with NBA All-Star Steph Curry." I told Dad later that it was probably the only time I would be considered in the same league with Steph Curry.

They went into the details of every facet of my life, and as they did, a new picture emerged as proof of their story. Mom's face was covered in tears. They had just walked her down memory lane—a street she loved to traverse. Using no notes, they relived the story of my life like it was a finely tuned dance. When they finished, pictures and videos speckled the wall, all representing my life.

They then asked me to come up to the wall and sign it with my finger. "Every athlete needs to sign the wall," they said. Dad wheeled me right next to it, turning my chair sideways, so I could use my working hand. My arm strained to reach, while my left pointer finger made its way straight out to get ready to sign. I wanted to make sure I could write in the best possible way. I knew my signature probably wouldn't look as beautiful as Michael Phelps's, Cam Newton's, or Lindsey Vonn's, but I was going to try. Very slowly, my hand began to sign "Johnny Agar." It took me awhile, but it was on the wall. Those months and years of struggling to write paid off right then. It probably was the sloppiest signature they'd ever received, but it was mine—and I was so proud it was up there.

Under Armour had told us they were able to get ESPN's Scott Van Pelt to moderate the Teammate Talk. SVP, as he was called, was an accomplished broadcaster who at the time hosted the late edition of *SportsCenter*. Our family knew of him well, as ESPN was on our TV all the time. Now Under Armour had provided us with the opportunity to chat with him for thirty minutes before taking the stage. We were extremely grateful for the opportunity.

Standing at about six foot six, SVP could be intimidating, but his warm presence and likable nature made us feel at ease seconds after being introduced to him. He was so personable and genuinely wanted to know more about us. Being a father to a brand-new little boy himself, he seemed in awe of what Dad did for me. "Your dad is pretty amazing, huh?" he looked at me and asked.

"Yeah, he could probably go a little faster," I quipped, waiting for Dad's retort. I wasn't disappointed. Dad came back with a flippant response: "Well, I might be a little faster, if you would stop eating those pastries over there and lose a little weight . . ."

We were bantering back and forth just like we did in our own family room at home. That's how comfortable SVP made us feel. He was gracious in answering a lot of career questions in the greenroom while we sat around the table that was adorned with fresh fruit—and what very few pastries were left.

After the talk, as we were sitting there chatting, the door to the back of the theater opened up, and in came Under Armour founder, Kevin Plank. Apparently, he kept texting the organizer of the event to "Keep Johnny there, I am en route." He was rushing back to headquarters to meet us.

I liked him a lot. I liked him because of what he represented, the underdogs, like me. Those people who have the odds stacked against them, yet keep going after their dream. Mr. Plank knows a lot about being the underdog because he was one himself. Ignored by recruiters, he had to fight for the opportunity to have a walk-on spot trying out for the University of Maryland football team his freshman year. Because of his grit, determination, and focus, he eventually became the special teams captain.

The same was true for his company. He knew his idea for a wicking shirt to wear under a uniform was a great idea, and selling out of his grandmother's basement, with only belief in himself and a dream, he turned his idea into what is now Under Armour.

"Really nice to meet you, partner. I am such a big fan of yours," Mr. Plank said, shaking my hand.

"I saw the quote where you said, 'You're smart enough to be naive enough to not know what you can accomplish,' and I think you really spoke to me when you said that. It's a tremendous inspiration to me."

He bent down so he could look me in the eye, and he put his left arm around me and held onto my hand with his right. He got closer and said, "You're a fighter. . . . You're a fighter. You define this company, and watching you perform is the heart and soul of everything I thought this company could be. Thank you for the inspiration you give to so many. You're a great man, and we love watching you and your dad."

Then Mr. Plank asked for a selfie with me—two underdogs who smiled for the camera. One who had the determination and grit to start a multibillion-dollar sports apparel corporation, and the other who pushed himself to have that same determination and grit in life—both of us sharing a picture, and a dream.

CHAPTER 13

[Will Finds a Way]

When I was about five years old, I remember being outside playing with Mom and Annie. Annie was riding on her shiny red tricycle, and Mom was pushing me in my black Ford F-150 ride-on truck. I remember watching Annie's legs pedal the bike. I was absorbed by the movement of her knees and legs, and loved watching her feet go up and down in a pattern of small circles. I decided I wanted to try that.

When we made it back to our house, as usual, Mom asked me where I wanted to go: on my lawn chair or on the grass. I responded with something different: "I wanna go on Annie's bike."

Surprised, Mom asked to clarify, "You want to sit on Annie's bike?"

I smiled and nodded my head slowly.

"Okay, we can try that," she said.

Mom sat me on the bike, but my body was woefully too rigid for its frame. My legs had a hard time bending to put my feet on the pedals, and when my feet did get there, my body pushed my butt back, forcing it to slide off the seat. It was clearly not going to work for me. I began to get frustrated.

Annie made it look so easy, I thought. Just then, Pa pulled up in our driveway. He could see the anguish on Mom's face and could see that I was disappointed. He quickly surmised that I wanted to ride Annie's bike, but it wasn't working. Mom and I showed Pa the challenge, and he came up with an idea. He purchased a green and yellow John Deere tractor tricycle for me. The frame was bigger than an average trike, and once he adapted the seat and the pedals, it fit my body perfectly.

I wanted to be on that bike all the time to learn how to go forward. Dad or Pa lifted the front end, so the wheel was off the pavement, and Mom made my legs move in a circular motion. Once I understood that, it got so Mom just pushed on the tops of my knees to help my legs move and help me to propel forward. Eventually, I was able to get just a slight push on my back to get me going.

One day, I kept pushing extremely hard with my feet by myself, until I made the bike go a half pedal forward. Mom encouraged me to keep my momentum going. I pushed hard again by myself, and my other leg made the same motion, except this time, I kept pedaling. I made it all the way down the driveway and started to go out in the street. I had done it. I could ride a bike.

I rode that bike everywhere I could; it made me feel good. I also rode it everywhere because I was proud that I had seen those kids riding in my neighborhood and willed myself to do the same.

I had persisted and taught myself how to do something. It was a lesson that I would remember time and time again as I got older.

UA ASSET

I got the call around Christmastime in 2017 that Under Armour wanted to feature me in their newest campaign called "Will Finds a Way." I was like George Bailey in the scene from *It's A Wonderful Life* when he finds out he had his life back again. I was hugging everyone and smiling and laughing. Christmas had come early for me—and I was so very grateful.

The campaign was going to star actor, producer, and semi-retired professional wrestler Dwayne "The Rock" Johnson and a handful of other "outrageously ambitious athletes" who set their sights high and showed the drive to go after them.

My family and I flew out to Los Angeles for the Under Armour shoot. When we arrived on the set, there were cars and trucks everywhere, and equipment was being hauled from one place to another. Everyone was moving like ants in an ant farm, continually on the go. We parked among the hundreds of vehicles and made our way to the main building, where it seemed all the action was. While watching one of the athletes film her spot, I looked to the left and saw a huge blackboard with small black-and-white animated pictures filling it. Above the board was a piece of paper that read "Our Cast—UA Assets" on it, with headshots of the people who were starring in the shoot. It was unreal to see a picture of me next to a headshot of Dwayne "The Rock" Johnson.

When a break in shooting came, a lady got up from her chair and came over to me. Her name was Carole McCarty. I knew exactly who she was: the senior producer of the film. She had a captivating personality and was full of energy and creativity, and although she was quite busy, she took the time to talk with us before heading back to the set.

Someone came to get us and told us that wardrobe would like to see us if we had a few minutes to spare. I smiled up at Dad because "wardrobe would like to see us." We both shook our heads in disbelief. She led us over to where there were coat racks upon coat racks of clothes. Annie and Gracy immediately gravitated over there. Instead of being separated by size, the clothes were separated by the names of the people in the film.

Just then, a woman came up to us and, bending over to greet me, said, "And you must be Johnny! I'm Priscilla. C'mon over here and let's try on some clothes to see how they fit you."

They decided the shirt was a little long for me, so they had the tailor come over. Dad was a "perfect large," so no tailoring needed for him.

ENCOUNTER

That night we hit the hay early, since we had to be up at three in the morning to get to the shooting location, which was about an hour away. The early morning couldn't come fast enough for me. My body was ready to go even before the alarm went off. Even Gracy was awake—and it was rare to see the whites of her eyes before at least ten in the morning.

Under Armour had wanted us to be there by 4:45 a.m., and we made it fifteen minutes early. The shooting location was an old, abandoned highway tucked away in the mountains. It was quite dark with no lights, except for one big spotlight that the crew had put up around their set. It was crazy to think they were all there and working so hard just to film me.

It's what you do in the dark that puts you in the light, I thought, and knew I was going to give it my all today for them. I didn't want to disappoint anyone.

While we waited, we were directed to a white trailer. Inside, we found breakfast foods and juice for us, as well as a cooler labeled "Johnny's Snacks." Before we left for LA, they had asked me about my favorite snacks and drinks, but I didn't realize why, until now. The cooler was filled with all my favorites: lemon-flavored vitaminwater, grape Propel, and chocolate milk, along with fresh pineapple and bananas. Mom popped inside the trailer to grab me a drink when a gentleman walked in the door.

"Good morning," the man said with a smile. "Are you part of the crew?"

"No," Mom responded, "I am actually the mom of Johnny— the guy who is going to be filmed today."

The gentleman was probably in his early sixties with glasses and graying hair. He had a bigger stature with broad shoulders and a tall frame. He took his glasses off and rubbed his eyes for a second before returning the glasses back over his nose. "Oh," he said, "I'm the driver for the crew. So, when they are filming your son, I will be driving the car alongside your son while the cameramen are shooting. What does your son do? Is he an athlete? You'll have to forgive me; I never know anything about what we are filming when I am called to work."

"Oh, that's okay! Actually, my son has cerebral palsy. He and my husband do races and triathlons together. My husband pushes and pulls him, and then my son gets up and walks the last mile with his walker," Mom said, beaming.

The man was quiet for a minute. His face lost its expression, and then suddenly he became very animated. "Wait a minute, is your husband about as tall as me and has brown . . ." his words were interrupted by Dad who had just walked in the door.

"That's him!" the man said, pointing at Dad.

Dad was caught a little off guard. Mom was just as perplexed as he was but explained to Dad that this man would be driving the car that carried the cameramen.

"Oh great, thank you for being here!" Dad said to him. "I'm Jeff."

"I know," he said. "I'm sorry, I'm Carl." The man looked like he had seen a ghost.

At that moment, Annie came in to tell Dad someone was looking for him to ask him a question about the walker. Dad excused himself and left the trailer.

"Is everything okay?" Mom asked Carl.

"Yes, I'm sorry. I'm just . . . this past weekend I was at a . . ."

You could tell he was struggling with how to approach what he was about to tell Mom. "I was at a meeting with some other guys for a couple of days."

"Oh, like a men's retreat?" Mom asked.

"Yes, that's exactly what it was. You're familiar with them?"

"Yes, actually, I've been on many retreats back in Michigan where I'm from. They're great to help you stay grounded in your faith," Mom said nonchalantly.

The man smiled.

"Well, my wife was pushing me to go to this retreat for weeks, and I was really dragging my feet not wanting to go. To make her happy, I finally decided to attend. The retreat was all about what it meant to be a good man and father to our children. It had been all right, but I still wasn't comfortable being there. I just was closed-off, not wanting to open up or make many friends while I was there, you know?"

He looked at Mom for acknowledgment. She nodded her head that she understood what he meant.

Carl continued, "In fact, I kept looking at my watch thinking of all the other things I could be doing rather than this.

But then they gathered all of us men, about two hundred of us, to watch a video . . . it was the *E:60* video about your son and husband.

"While we watched it, I started to see grown men cry, so moved by the relationship your husband and son had together. I began to cry as well. Something about watching that changed me. I called my wife right after seeing it, thanking her for making me come to this."

Carl began to get tears in his eyes. "She had been praying hard for me and my relationship with my son, and we feel like your video, your son and husband's example, was exactly what we needed . . . what I needed."

Tears started flowing down Mom's eyes. She gave Carl a hug and thanked him.

"You know, I was trying to decide if I was going to take this job or not," he said. "Because I had been on the Men's Encounter all weekend, it put me behind on my to-do list at home. I was sitting at a red light, on the phone with them trying to decide, when a huge semitruck pulled up beside me and on the side of it, it had the word, 'Encounter.' I took that as a sign, and I'm so glad I did!"

He smiled really big now and continued, "I know some people will think this is all coincidental—but not me, my wife is too persistent when it comes to praying for her family!"

Mom added, "I like to call them 'God-incidences.'" They both laughed.

It was going to be a great day, Mom thought.

"THAT'S A WRAP!"

Aside from the frigid cold weather, it was a great day. It was in the low forties in the morning, and I was worried that my legs might give me a hard time moving. However, I was so pumped up with adrenaline, I barely felt a difference. Between every shot, Mom or one of the producers wrapped a blanket around me to keep me warm.

The sun was just rising over the mountains, painting the sky with spectacular colors that were beautiful to the naked eye and even more gorgeous on camera. It was exactly what the producer wanted. At one point, she became emotional when she saw the morning sky serving as a backdrop to me walking. "This is just an amazing shot," she kept saying, tearful over what she was seeing.

Just then, a California condor, with beautiful outstretched wings, glided through the shot, leaving its parting call as it flew past us overhead. Carole yelled out, "Aww, man! I hope you guys got that in the shot!"

They did, and everyone cheered. "That's a wrap, everyone!" Carole called. It couldn't have been scripted any better.

We had been at that location for about three hours, and now it was on to another location at a gym, about forty-five minutes away. I knew they had wanted me to do some pull-ups, so I put them into my training routine and worked on them dutifully before heading out to California. The gym was set up for gymnasts, with big springy floor mats everywhere. Under Armour was also filming Javon "Wanna" Walton there. Wanna was a boxing and gymnast prodigy at eleven years old. It was amazing to watch him do back flips and somersaults in his floor routine with such ease.

They had brought in a special pull-up weight machine for my part of the shoot. Once it was set up, I changed clothes and was introduced to my stunt coordinator, T. J. Slaughter. T.J. had been drafted in the third round in 2000 by the Jacksonville Jaguars but was now working his way into the film industry. He was a massively built man with the greenest eyes I had ever seen. Originally from Alabama, his Southern charm and manners won a lot of people over, including my family. We got along really well as I joked with him that he would be a better stunt double for me because we looked so much alike!

T.J. was there to help Dad position me on the pull-up bar and then step away for the shot. When I was done, he helped get me down. They would yell, "Action!" and that was my cue to pull myself up. I heard a lot of "ohhs and ahhs" and knew they liked the shots they were getting—so I worked harder.

When I couldn't do anymore, I let Dad and T.J. know I was letting go and they came over and got me. It was a great system and was working out well, until I forgot to tell them I was letting go . . . I went down onto the mat hearing a unison of gasps as I made my way down. To which I immediately popped my head up from the mat and said, "I'm good—I just wanted you to see my floor routine!" Everyone laughed.

It was time to say our good-byes. We got a group shot before heading out, and I thanked everyone profusely for allowing me to be a part of this whole campaign. I was so very grateful for the opportunity to represent Under Armour and asked them to please forward my gratitude onto the folks at Droga5, the advertising firm that handled the project, as well—especially founder David Droga, who I heard requested me for this campaign. Amazed that he would consider me to represent both his company and Under Armour's advertising campaign, I was stunned and so, so very thankful.

I thought back to that time when I learned how to ride my bike and was glad I had willed myself to stick with it.

IMPACT

I was so blessed to have people in my life who encouraged me and helped me learn to shut down the naysayers, and to stay strong when the odds were against me. Those people showed me the way and taught me how to hope for the future and dream big. And when I walked my impossible mile, it quickly became apparent that I was able to do the same for at least one other person. The gray-haired gentleman with the prosthetic leg showed me that. I had given him a glimmer of hope—and that felt extremely good.

After the *E:60* feature aired, I started to see the impact of my accomplishment on a lot of other people as well, and I was completely taken aback by it. I never anticipated touching so many people in so many different ways. I was hearing from people in the

United States and all over the world: Saudi Arabia, Puerto Rico, Brazil, China, Canada, England, Ethiopia, even the Marshall Islands, and they were all telling me the same thing—if I had the courage, then they could face their struggles too.

Several months after the show was aired, Dad and I had signed up to do the Riverbank Run again. The day before the race, there was an expo where different companies and nonprofits would set up shop to show off their products or raise awareness.

My whole family had gone, and we had just picked up our race packet, when we heard a gasp, and someone yelled from quite a distance away, "Johnny Agar!" When we looked to the left in the direction the voice had come from, we saw a red-haired woman with a ponytail, half running, half walking up to me with arms outstretched. By the time she reached me, she was sobbing and laughing and smiling all at once and had her arms around my neck and shoulders hugging me tightly. She was not going to let go anytime soon.

I looked at Mom and Dad waiting for them to mouth to me who this woman was, but they looked just as perplexed as I did. Annie and Gracy weren't able to give me any clues either and just shrugged their shoulders.

Right about that time, the woman slowly began to pull away from me, almost as if she had just realized she was in a public place and may have been squeezing me too hard. As she tried to gain her composure, she backed up and began to apologize, still gasping for breaths between her spaced-out words.

"I'm . . . so . . . sorry," she sniffled. "I just can't believe it. You all probably think I have lost it!" she said, starting to smile.

Mom looked at her and rubbed her back a little, letting her know she was not being judged.

She continued, "About a year ago, I went to see my doctor. I was overweight, my blood pressure was through the roof, I had bad back problems, I was prediabetic, and all I did was sit on the couch because I just didn't care anymore. The doctor said, 'Regina, if you don't do something to change your life around, you are going to die at a very early age.' He said I was basically killing myself by sitting there doing nothing."

She began to cry again, and Mom reached over and gave her a small hug.

Regina continued with her story. "I was sitting on the couch one day, and Johnny, your story came on the TV about how you had always wanted to be an athlete and had decided to walk a mile. You talked about taking things step by step, not going too fast, just taking things baby step by baby step, and at that moment, something inside me clicked. I thought, *If he can walk a mile, I can certainly walk out to the mailbox to get the mail.* And that's how I started. I walked out to the mailbox that day, and I would walk a little farther down the street the next day, and a little farther the next day. I did that every day because of you! And now, tomorrow, I'm going to participate in the 5K walk of the Riverbank Run.

"I saw my doctor the other day, and he was amazed at how much better I was doing. My blood pressure was down, I was losing weight, I didn't have to take as much medicine as I had been, and I began doing exercises for my back . . . you saved my life, Johnny."

Tears were flowing heavily now from my new friend, Regina, and from each one of us.

During that race, Dad and I had about an eighth of a mile to go. I had been walking the last mile and was about three-hundred feet from the finish line when I heard, "Johnny!" It was Regina. She was just finishing up her 5K. She made her way over to us and asked if she could walk with us across the finish line. I said I would love nothing more. She put her hand on top of mine, and we walked together across the finish line.

We had not come in first. We had not gotten any prize money, but we each gained something we will never ever forget— for Regina it was her life back, and for me, it was a newfound perspective.

UNBELIEVABLE

One afternoon, we received a call from an unknown number.

"Hello, is this a Mr. Jeffrey?" the voice with a Japanese accent said.

"Hi, no, this is his wife, Becki. May I help you?"

"Ahh, yes. I am a Mr. Hideo Nagano, and I am from the TV show *Unbelievable* here in Japan. It is a documentary TV show.

The show's producers, ah, had seen Johnnysan's *E:60* feature on ESPN and wanted to feature his story on our show."

"Wow! That's amazing!" I replied, now on the phone with Mom.

"Ah, we were wondering, ah, if we could send some people out with the camera and film the family while we ask the questions to you?"

"Absolutely," Mom responded, "that would be wonderful!"

When we got off the phone, Mom's eyes were glistening. She turned to me and said, "Johnny, what a great chance this gives you to help change people's perceptions. Just think, you may end up helping someone on the other side of the world to have a more positive outlook on life."

It was amazing to think that I could help someone change the course of their life for the better.

The folks from Japan came in for two days to film and interview us. They had a translator come with them. When everything was done, they told us they would send us a copy of the tape, so we could see what they created. Dad had worked with a person who was from Japan, and when she found out we were going to be on *Unbelievable,* she was amazed. It was apparently the hottest show on Japanese TV.

Several weeks later, we received a DVD in the mail from Hideo. Although the show was completely in Japanese, we were altogether surprised when we saw they had hired actors to portray our family. They reenacted our lives, even having our family's pictures in frames on the table and on the walls in the house. It was crazy to watch.

Mom's character looked like the beautiful Gwyneth Paltrow, while Dad jokingly said his character looked more like Kronk from one of our favorite Disney movies, *The Emperor's New Groove*.

Every now and then, just to get his goat a little, we answered him with a line from one of Kronk's scenes, "Squeaker squeak squeak squeaken," and laughed hysterically.

"BLOODY AMAZING"

When we were in Kona in 2016, I was feeling pretty down after not finishing the race and apologized to Mom for not giving everyone the outcome they had wanted. Dad was sitting next to her and looked down when I said that. You could tell it was heavy on his heart as well.

Mom looked at me and smiled. She said, "Unfortunately, you guys were unable to experience what we did because you were training or out on the course."

I looked at her questioningly. "What do you mean?" I asked.

"Johnny, remember what you told us after you walked at St. Pat's? How happy you were to find out that your walk meant something to other people too?"

I nodded and slowly smiled.

"Well, being here, participating in this race has done the same—and you didn't even know it.

"Remember when you and Dad decided to take a practice swim a couple of days ago and I was waiting for you both at the sea wall?"

That day Ironman allowed participants to get their feet wet by allowing them to swim part of the actual swim course. Because of that, hundreds of people had lined the shore and sat atop the sea wall, sitting and watching athletes swim out and back. It was a beautiful thing, really. Most everyone there came from different parts of the globe, with different cultures and different languages, and while we may not have been able to understand each other, we all belonged to the same family—Ironman.

Mom continued, "When I was out there waiting for you, the neatest thing happened. I saw and heard many people who were just amazed at what they were seeing. They would stop me and ask in their broken English if you were going to participate in the race, as they pointed to you and Dad. 'Yes,' I would say, and they would either put their hands up to their mouth in amazement, start crying, or give me a hug."

Dad's head came up to look at me.

"Anyway," she went on, "as I was standing there watching you swim out, I overheard a conversation from a couple from England. The husband had just finished his practice swim and came up to his wife who had her eyes fixed on your dad and you out in the water. Winded, he said to his wife, 'Love, how'd I do?'

"'Honey,' she said, 'I just saw something so bloody amazing! Remember that father/son team we read about who are going to be participating in the race on Saturday? I just saw them go out in the boat. They are out there now. See them?' And she pointed to where you guys were."

Mom was trying to use her best British accent and continued telling the story. "The husband said, 'That's great dear, but . . .' She then interrupted him and said, 'Darling,' as she began to cry, 'they were just incredible. Watching him get his son into the boat so gently—and to think he is going to pull him the whole way.' The lady wiped her eyes with a Kleenex.

"'Yes, but darling,' her husband became exasperated, 'how did *I* do? You were supposed to have been timing me? Did you stop the watch when I came out?'

"She looked down at the watch and hit the stop button. Keeping her eyes fixed on your boat in the water, she said, 'So sorry, love. I just got so wrapped up in watching them, I forgot about you out there swimming. Look, they're on their way back in . . .'"

We were amazed and laughed at the sweetness of the story, but Mom wasn't finished yet. "That's not all. When you guys were out on the bike course, the most amazing thing happened. Remember we all went into that restaurant next to the course to eat some breakfast?

"We all sat down, and our waitress came over to give us some water. She looked at me curiously like she knew me but didn't say anything. Then, when she came back to take our order, she set an extra pitcher of water down and walked around to where I was sitting. She bent down and softly said, 'Are you Mrs. Agar?'

"I looked at her trying to quickly remember if I knew her from somewhere.

"'I am!' I said.

"She said her name was Beth and apologized. 'I'm sorry, you don't know me.'

"I could tell she was nervous. Then she said to me, 'I have been watching your son and husband all week out here practicing together. I saw them at the shore when they went for their practice swim. I was working, but we were slow that morning, and I watched them together.' Then Beth started to cry and couldn't speak for a few moments."

As Mom was explaining what happened, she teared up as she struggled to get the story out. "Then the waitress said, 'I just wanna say that I have two young boys and I thought I had to work to make more money for them for extras, ya know? So, I've been working, taking on two shifts here at the restaurant,' she sniffed.

"'I just want you to know that when I saw your son and husband out there in the water, I realized the time I spend with my sons is way more important than the extra money. That's why, last night, I quit my second shift job, so I could spend more time with them. Your family showed me what was more important, and I wanted to thank you for that.'"

Mom, with tears running down her face, looked me in the eye and squeezed my hand. Then she said, "So, while the outcome may not have been what you wanted for this race, it was definitely what others needed. Don't ever be sorry for that. You helped encourage people to see things from a different perspective and helped motivate them to do better."

In looking back, I know I will never get to stand out on the mound to throw a perfect game or catch a Hail Mary pass in the end zone. I would never be as great an athlete as the ones I looked up to all my life. But, I at least felt good knowing my struggles and challenges gave hope to others, and that no matter how rocky their road, they realized they were all capable of walking their own impossible mile.

CHAPTER 14

[Ready to Live]

It took a team to handle everything we took on with racing, which included well over one hundred races—and still counting—and each of us had our own role to play. Dad trained hard to get me to that finish line so I could walk across it. He was my coach, and my role model. Aunt Janet and Uncle Chris supported me in my training with walking, but they did more than that; they were there to make me laugh, calm my fears, and let me cry on their shoulder when I didn't want Mom or Dad to know my fears. While Uncle John and I no longer share F-150 rides with milkshakes in our hands, and my fish tank is long gone, he is still the first person I call with good news—or if I just need someone to talk to.

Terence traveled with us and was invaluable for Dad, both in race prep and helping to calm Dad's nerves. They were very much alike in that they both loved lists and were very methodical, so they worked well together. My sisters watched the dynamics of the family and filled in where it was needed and served as the support crew—carrying, hauling, packing, and helping . . . always helping. My cousins were our cheerleaders and provided hugs and laughter, and ice cream, when we needed it most.

People often think it is my dad who is the most vital member of our team. After all, he is the motor. But if Dad is the motor, Mom is the whole car. She takes care of everything else: the logistics, scheduling, marketing, communication, sponsorships, coordination, and the maintenance of our whole team—our whole family. She is the unsung hero of the group, and she is all right with that.

Her ultimate goal is, and always will be, to be there when needed, to nurture, to love. Please don't mistake this for weakness. It was Mom who encouraged us to go down to the finish line after failing at Kona because "it would be good for us." She was right. When we found out our spare chariot wheel was delayed in shipping to Germany for the DATEV Challenge Roth, it was Mom who ran from home to home in a little German village looking for anyone who would give up a wheel on their child's bike. She found one. It was Mom who arranged the luggage in such a way so Gracy could lay down on our nineteen-hour drive to the Ironman Texas, even though it meant sacrificing her own legroom. She never complained.

Mom is definitely the strongest member of our family. If love were measured in horsepower, she could push every one of us—at the same time—across an Ironman finish line. Her fuel and drive is her faith. And her motivation? The love she has for all of us. It is her conviction and her guidepost.

When you can have somebody who can take the experiences of her life and turn them into a positive, and look at everything with such an optimistic attitude, it provides the team with a cohesiveness that can transform any challenge we face. She reminds us what the right perspective in life is. We are the body, but Mom is the heartbeat and the oxygen of the team.

Years ago at the age of nineteen, sitting in a small hospital room in the Bahamas, my mom watched her own mother die. My mom told me it was extremely difficult for her. Her mother had been her best friend, her confidant, her critic, her consoler, her teacher— and she didn't know how she was going to go on with such a void in her life. She had already lost her brother—her only sibling— four years earlier, and now to lose her mom was inconceivable.

When she asked a good friend if anyone would be able to fill that void again, the friend gave her one of the best answers. She said no one person would be able to occupy it—she would have to find many people to fill the space. She would have to build a team around her. She needed someone to take on each role that my grandma had once given her. What's amazing is that I was the beneficiary of that advice. My mom says it was my gift from my grandma Ann.

When I was born with so many complications and with an outcome of cerebral palsy, my mom knew she had to have a good team to support me, to influence me, to help me grow into the man she knew I could become. And Dad knew the importance of teamwork through his sports career. He knew that the player was only as good as the rest of the team. Mom and Dad together made the perfect team for me. They taught me the basics but gave me the most important foundation.

A couple of years later my team grew when my sisters were born. They became my encouragers. Slowly with each passing year, I added more players to my team. They were in the friendships I built along the way, in the schools I attended, and in the communities where I lived. My team grew as I grew. I became stronger because of the people who surrounded me and loved me—like Pa. I think back to his only wish in his last days: to see Johnny Boy walk. *I'm doing it, Pa, I'm walking. I know you're still a part of my team Upstairs.*

I know that everything I have achieved was because of the people who supported me, taught me, and loved me. I know exactly what Mom's friend meant when she said Mom had to be surrounded by many to fill the void of one.

By myself, I am just whistling a tune, but with my parents, I add a brass section, giving me the confidence and power I need. My sisters become my percussion—keeping me in rhythm and adding excitement to my life; my friends become my woodwinds section—often taking on a supporting role and providing the harmony; and my community becomes the strings section—the most numerous of the groups who help carry the melody.

When we all work together, we form a hardworking and harmonious orchestra—ready to play the beautiful symphony that is my life with the Great Conductor as the lead.

TAKING THE MOUND

I think back on a lot of things in my life, and the impact they have had on me, and wonder if I could have ever imagined my future.

There's a scene I play in my mind all the time.

I'm in Heaven—and the scene happens right before I'm born. It takes place at a perfect baseball diamond, and I'm standing on the pitching mound.

"Johnny!" an angel jogs out to the mound to greet me.

We smile and fist bump. We've known each other forever.

"Johnny, I need to tell you something."

"Sure," I say. "What's up? You're not takin' me out of the game, are you? I was just getting warmed up!"

"Johnny," the angel says, "you're going to be born with cerebral palsy."

I can't believe what I'm hearing.

"But don't worry," she says quickly, "we're going to equip you with a family who will stick with you, and believe in you. With a real team."

"But I want to be an athlete," I protest. "Will my parents help me?"

The angel smiles knowingly. I've seen her smile infinite times before, but this time it's different somehow. Wiser, maybe. Like she's just answered me, even though she hasn't.

"But what if I can't do it?" I ask. "What if I fail?"

"If?" she asks me. She puts a hand on my shoulder. "Johnny, it's not *if*, it's *when*. That's part of what it means to be human."

I look down.

"But Johnny?" she gets my attention again, gently lifting my chin. "Remember that team I mentioned? Your family is going to teach you how to get back up again whenever you fall. And you'll learn how to laugh at yourself when you do."

I look around the ballpark. Around Heaven. The idea of leaving and going to Earth is almost too much to bear. I look back at the angel.

"Will . . . will I make it?"

"You will. You will, Johnny," she promises. "As long as you stay determined, you'll make it. As long as you believe, you'll make it."

"But I'm scared."

"Of course you are!" she says. "And your fear is part of what will drive you. Always remember, always believe, that God has a plan for you. A good and perfect plan that you can't yet imagine. And your life is going to help other people live."

I take a deep breath of perfect heavenly air. I ask the angel another question. "But what if I can't always stay determined— what if I don't always believe?"

"That's part of being human too, Johnny," she answers, "and part of the reason we're equipping you with this particular family. They'll help you believe, Johnny. And they'll show you that love can overcome any obstacle."

I'm silent, thinking it all over. At last I ask, "How can I know it'll happen like that?"

"You can't yet," the angel says, smiling her wise smile again. "The only way to know is to live it, Johnny."

I take one last breath. I take the angel's hand. "Okay," I say, "I'm ready to live."

And then I'm born. I open my eyes. The scene is over.

You would think it was a dream . . . a leap of the imagination so unbelievable that most people would call it pure fantasy.

Yet, here I am. I look around and am surrounded by Mom, Dad, and my sisters. My faith in God fills my heart. And I know the scene I imagine isn't a dream. Or not only a dream. It's my reality.

It's why, when people say to me, "God bless you," I often think to myself, *He already has.*

ACKNOWLEDGMENTS

MY SIGNPOSTS

This road I have walked hasn't always been smooth, and I haven't always been able to see where I am going clearly. Fortunately, there have been many signposts along the way that have guided me down the right path and have steered me clear of rocky or uneven ground. When there have been forks in the road, I have been blessed with bright glow-in-the-dark signs showing me which path to choose. These signposts have been the people in my life who have encouraged me, stayed with me, guided me, and helped me along my road through life. They are a part of this book just as much as I am.

At the root of these signposts are two very special people: Mom and Dad. While my dad has always supported me in reaching for my dreams, he also pushes me past the barriers that most people would have stopped me at—and then he pushes me a little more. Always doing so with the love a father has for his son.

The mom I have been blessed with is fiercely faithful to God and her family, and I'm so grateful for her loving arms that have held me when I needed it most. Her optimism in seeing my potential helped me see what was possible.

My life would be less beautiful and far less glittery without my sisters to decorate it with laughter and lipstick. They were my first friends and will always be my best friends. Having a brother with cerebral palsy has not made it easy on them: the many hours of sitting through PT, OT, and speech therapy, the numerous hospital stays, and the endless tears I shed when I couldn't process anything anymore and I was worn down by life. I hope I can make it up to you a thousandfold. (The Under Armour private jet to Texas was a good start, wasn't it?!) My sisters have always been there to pick me back up again, make me smile, or tell me to be quiet because Dad had lost his patience and was going to come in and send us all to bed.

To my sister Annie. Thank you for being the athlete I always aspired to be. As a catcher, you were never afraid of taking on one of the most important positions on the diamond and weren't afraid of getting beaten down by the ball or bat—always coming through under pressure—all the things I needed to see in life. Thank you for your steady hand of guidance, ever ready and always appreciated. Even though we didn't always see eye to eye on the teams we rooted for (Go Green! Go Lions!) I was always and will always be falling out of my chair rooting for you.

To my sister Gracy. You danced your way into all of our hearts the minute we laid eyes on you and have been dancing on mine ever since. Sometimes your steps can be soft and graceful on my heart as your name suggests—like when you see me struggling to brush my hair and come over to style it with your own trendy design. Sometimes your steps can be more like a heavy hip-hop, and we clash because of our nine-year age difference. But through it all, you have shown me what it means to be empathetic toward others, to show kindness to those who need it most, and to muster up enough strength even when you feel like quitting. You have shown me the paradox of what it looks like to be tough and soft all at the same time, and I am so grateful for that.

Collaborator. Helper. Defender. Storyteller. Teacher. Grandma. Thank you, Grandma, for making me always feel that I could do anything. For meeting your friends for breakfast every week and taking up most of the conversation with pictures of me and bragging about the most recent milestone I had hit. Thank you for writing the scathing letter to my teacher when I was four. You told her not to count me out just because I wasn't able to concentrate fully on a task when I "was a whiz at the computer, knows his telephone number and address, plus much more, should he be labeled as not being able to pay attention?" Yes, I still have that letter . . . and thank you for not sending it. Thank you for filling me in on all the details of Dad's life growing up. You always believed in the power of me. I am truly grateful and will always love you for that.

Grandpa, every year I look forward to getting on the phone with you for three hours and picking teams for our bowl pick. Thank you for reading the stats with me and studying the teams, even though you probably knew everything I had just read to you about them anyway. And thank you for your patience in having to do it all over again because my computer timed out since I typed so slowly. Every year I look forward to failing miserably with you again at our losing choices. Thank you for talking to me about sports . . . any sport. It is so gratifying to know there is someone out there who loves sports just as much as I do, and that he's my grandpa. And thank you for marrying Grandma Paula. She helped breathe life into you, and her simple acts of kindness toward all of us have been greatly appreciated. But most importantly, thank you for teaching me what it means to love unconditionally.

Pa, you were only in my life for four short years but taught me enough for a lifetime. Thank you for keeping your fridge stocked with Jell-O chocolate puddings and bait so I could hold onto those memories and pull them out when I needed them most. I will never forget how, even when you were on your deathbed, your heartrate on the monitors would go up when Mom mentioned my name. You never got the chance to see me walk, and I know you wanted to stay with me here to see that, but I know you will always be walking along beside me helping to lighten my steps . . . especially when I'm on my way to cheer for MSU basketball during March Madness. Go Green! (From Heaven, "Go White, Johnny Boy!") Oh, and please say "hi" to Joltin' Joe for me up there, will ya?

Grandma Ann, although I never met you, I feel you almost every day and see you when my mother smiles at me. Thank you for raising Mom to be the person she is today. I know it's you who comes to visit me out on the mound in my dreams.

Uncle John. I am so proud to carry your name. When I was researching information for this book, I would ask "Dad, wasn't it you who helped support the family by working a lot of hours?" "No," he would say, "that was your uncle John."

"Well, didn't you help Grandma out a lot?"

"Not really, that was more your uncle John."

Not surprisingly, you would have given the shirt off your back to anyone. Thank you for teaching me that there is nothing more important than the time spent with the people you love. Thank you for being there for me when I just needed to have a chat, needed a "pick-me-up," and for holding my fingers when I was hurting through all my surgeries. Without you, my life would be filled with less laughter, fewer fish, fewer milkshake calories, less kite flying, less time in an F-150, less time out on the water, and less love. Thank you for showing me what it means to be a "John" the family can be proud of.

To Aunt Kathy and Uncle Rick, thank you for accepting the challenge to take care of me for many weekends so Dad and Mom could get a much-needed break, even when you had no clue what you were doing. With no kids and newly married, you opened up your hearts and schedule to a little boy who had some different challenges. Thank you for spending time with me. For zooming me through the air, playing catch with me, our trips to Mackinac Island, Williamsburg, and SeaWorld, and for taking me out onto the softball field during Traverse City tournaments to either run the bases or field balls. All of those things helped in making me feel as typical a little boy as was possible. You have always supported me and been happy for me with each endeavor I have taken on, and I am so thankful for you both.

A special thanks to Aunt Janet and Uncle Chris. Now I know what it looks like to give of yourself until you feel like you can't give anymore—and then find out there is so much more you can do. Thank you for the unlimited supply of vitaminwater, Reese's Peanut Butter Cups, showers after workouts, and kisses and love. Thank you also for giving me cousins—Emily, Mary, and Lily—who are the best at making up cheers and cheering me on. Aunt Janet, thank you for dropping everything to come stretch out my legs because I had a pain in my quad, and for being there at every practice walk to take blurry videos so I could not post them on Instagram. You put up with my constant puns, some of which are really bad, and yet still love me. Thank you for staying true to your high school senior slogan: "Janet, Janet, Best on the Planet!"

Uncle Chris, thank you for being the voice of reason for me when I felt like I was going to "jump ship" many times—especially while flying in an airplane. You placing your arms tightly around me on the plane ride home from Germany made me feel safe and secure—just as your presence in my life does all the time. Thank you for the trips to BW3's to watch the game and eat their wings (a LOT of their wings!), as well as being ready with your fishing pole both in the winter and summer for me.

Terence, thank you for playing such a pivotal role in the growth of my life and in making the road I walked much easier; by helping me to soar on the wings of angels with myTeam Triumph, you allowed Dad to see what was possible and helped to form TeamAgar. Your knowledge, coupled with your South African accent and more tranquil nature, is a great addition to TeamAgar. Thank you for being such an awesome equipment guru, a calming voice for Dad, a timekeeper for Mom, and a great friend to us all.

I will be forever thankful to you, Andrea Dear, for having the faith to see my potential at the very young age of four. You have not just watched me grow up, but you have also been a large part of my every day. You taught me how to use my body to its potential, while also teaching me how to be responsible, mature, kind, strong, and brave, and making sure I did all those things while keeping my feet flat, holding my hands, and keeping my elbows at my sides. I'd like to say I was special, but the reality is you treat everyone with the same love, kindness, and gentleness, and with the same undying trust we all have for you. *Szeretlek drágám.*

The conductive education program at the Conductive Learning Center of North America in Grand Rapids, Michigan, taught me at an early age how to set goals and go after them with hard work, discipline, and focus. It also showed me that it was two hundred times better when you were surrounded by friends who encouraged and motivated you to reach your goal. Thank you, Gyuri, for being there every step of the way to document not just my journey, but also everyone's, through photos and videos— probably realizing that years from now we each would find it hard to believe the amount of progress we were able to attain through the program. Thank you so much to my friends-turned-family there. *Mindannyian különlegesek vagytok!*

Dr. Batton, while I don't remember meeting you in the hospital when I was first born, it was a pleasure talking to you on the phone recently to thank you personally for helping my parents take the first step on this long, winding road that is my life. Your advice paved the way toward who I am and was the reason I was able to write this book.

My faith has always been a big part of who I am, but Fr. Mark Peacock, you have strengthened it even more. You walked with me physically that first mile but will walk with me spiritually for the rest of my life.

To my St. Patrick family, you have prayed for me, supported me, and cheered for me with each small step I made. I will never forget that.

Clare, you started out as a student at Aquinas learning about my disability, became my babysitter, turned into my teacher/conductor, became my friend—and became my best friend when you decided to call ESPN about my one-mile walk! Without you making that call, this book would be a pile of scattered pages about someone who one day decided to do something hard.

Mom always wanted to have a saint in the family, and she was happy she finally got one when I became an Aquinas College Saint! To my Aquinas family, especially all the professors who encouraged me to write this book, thank you for always being accepting of me, even if it meant having to rearrange the classroom to accommodate my chair. You taught me so much more than what just comes out of a book, and I hope I make you proud to call me an alumnus! Go Saints!

Justin Verlander, you helped a young boy dream without even knowing it and shaped his life to mimic yours out on the mound. Thank you for serving as an inspiration to me. Can't wait to see you in the Hall of Fame someday. The number thirty-five will look great next to all the other baseball legends! And I will still be wearing the number proudly on my back.

Michael Phelps, the odds of participating in the Olympics are .0013 percent. You swam in five. The odds of winning a gold medal at any one of them is .00001 percent—you have earned twenty-three. It's staggering to look at it that way. While it is a feat no one has ever accomplished, it is not the reason I look up to you. It's the man behind the gold medals that motivates me— the person you are, not the swimmer. The one who gave it his all because he knew he could accomplish anything he wanted. The one who knew the hard work had to be put in if he wanted to reach his goal. The one who got weighed down by the demands of the world, refocused, and came out swinging again. Thank you, Michael, for allowing me to swim in the wake you created. You made it easier for me to keep my head above water in my own swim lane called life. For that, I will be eternally grateful.

Mr. Plank and Under Armour, your story is one of resilience, grit, determination, and resolve, and your spirit to succeed burns brighter than ever. Thank you for seeing in me the same qualities your company started with and still has. I promise I will always try to "walk with a purpose."

Droga5 and Mr. Droga, you make a living by putting things out there that have the opportunity to take on a greater life and make a huge impact. I am here to tell you thank you for that. The "Rule Yourself" Under Armour ad fueled me to keep going when I wanted to quit. Thank you for having faith in me to try to do the same in the "Will Finds a Way" campaign. I hope I made you proud.

Scott Van Pelt, to the Man of the Midnight Hour, thank you for rooting for me and for your willingness to be the "sixth man" on the Agar team.

Finally, to all those who have had a part in the road I have walked: to my many therapists, especially Kim Gleason for being both tough and sweet on me; Bev Chesebro and Donna Crowl for your kindness (and strong legs!); and RunGR crew for helping us to conquer hills and holding us accountable. Thanks to my first team; Chad and Beth Spaman for introducing me to myTeam Triumph (and introducing Dad to ocean swimming and stingrays!); Mike Bieker for giving me the chance to see the details of the back of a pace car; and Phil Vanderlugt for being our fastest anchor. To Rob Jackson and his team at Extra Credit Projects for helping to tell my story, and to Greg Meyer and Greg McAleenan, who looked at a kid in a wheelchair who was asking whether he could ever be a sponsored athlete and immediately responded "yes" and put me on my road toward Kona.

ACKNOWLEDGMENTS

None of what we have been able to do would have been possible without people and organizations who believed in us.

I have great memories of Fred and Lena Meijer coming to the Conductive Learning Center and sharing stories to encourage us. Their visits were always a blessing. It was their funding of the center that helped me learn to walk, and years later I was proud to have them as a primary sponsor for walking in races. I view that as a wonderful full circle. It's a chance to celebrate everything I've grown and learned to be with their help. Mr. Meijer always used to tell me to "keep working hard." I'm grateful that he gave me the opportunity to keep doing that.

To all my sponsors: Amway, Adaptive Star, Zipp, SRAM, Ironman, Cycles Chinook, Rifton, Music That Moves, Roka, Giant Bicycles, Rudy Project, Aquinas College, Herman Miller, Northern Cross Foundation, Equest Center for Therapeutic Riding, Lacks Enterprises, Advanced Elements, Ingalls Pictures, Extra Credit Projects. Thank you for removing the barriers on the road that would have blocked my path to reach my dream.

PUBLISHING ACKNOWLEDGMENTS

Our team believed in us and came together like the elements of a comforting book.

Thank you, Tom Dean, for acting as our book cover—catching everyone's attention with your brilliant yet humble hues of color and encouraging them to want to know more about our story. Thank you for believing in us.

To Dexterity Books, as the binding of our book, you assembled and secured a great team to surround us, bringing our message to life. Thank you for the passion you put into our story.

Lastly, to our editor Rebecca Nordquist, we had the words, but you helped develop them into a beautiful story. In our style sheet under "R" it would read: "Rebecca—master of grammar, friend to Johnny and Becki." Thank you for your kindness.

ABOUT THE AUTHORS

Johnny Agar gained international attention when he walked a mile in his church's annual 5K. That sounds like an odd reason for fame, except for the reality of Johnny's severe cerebral palsy. Even with a lifetime of physical therapy before this race, the longest distance he'd ever previously walked was twenty-three steps.

Since that incredible feat, Johnny and his father, Jeff, have partnered in countless races, including the infamous Ironman World Championship in Kona, Hawaii, which was chronicled by NBC. Johnny has been featured on *Today*, *Inside Edition*, *NBC Nightly News*, *People*, *USA Today*, *HuffPost*, and ESPN's *SportsCenter* and *E:60*. His tenacity and indelible spirit have inspired numerous professional and Olympic athletes, and Johnny is a brand ambassador for the sports apparel company Under Armour. Even so, he will tell you that his crowning accomplishment was getting post-race recognition from his biggest sponsor in the form of twenty gallons of his favorite Meijer ice cream.

Now Johnny gives motivational speeches to inspire others to overcome their challenges and chase their dreams, one step at a time. Among his other roles, Johnny serves as the athletic ambassador for the Cerebral Palsy Foundation, and he's proud to have earned a dual major in sports management and business administration from Aquinas College in Grand Rapids, Michigan.

Becki Agar is an advocate, philanthropist, and mother of three children. After Becki began a career as a credit analyst, her passion for children led her to open a day care. When she had children of her own, she closed the day care to raise them, an experience that has been the greatest blessing of her life.

Becki fundraises and advocates for organizations that have been instrumental in helping children who have special needs to be as independent as possible on their journeys through life. She graduated from Grand Valley State University with a degree in sociology and a minor in psychology.

The Impossible Mile is Johnny and Becki's first book.